DERBYSHIRE

of one hundred years ago

HATHERSAGE

THE GAMEKEEPERS AT CALKE ABBEY

DERBYSHIRE

of one hundred years ago

DAVID BUXTON

Budding
BOOKS

A Budding Book

First published in the United Kingdom in 1992 by
Alan Sutton Publishing Limited, an imprint of Sutton Publishing Limited
Phoenix Mill · Thrupp · Stroud · Gloucestershire

This edition first published in 1998 by Budding Books,
an imprint of Sutton Publishing Limited

A catalogue record for this book is available from the British Library.

ISBN 1 84015 086 6

MATLOCK BATH

Typeset in 11/13 Bembo.
Typesetting and origination by
Sutton Publishing Limited.
Printed in Great Britain by
WBC Limited, Bridgend, Mid-Glamorgan.

Preface

In *Derbyshire of one hundred years ago* I have tried to recreate on the page some of the appearance and the atmosphere of the county in the late nineteenth century. Old photographs provide the visual images of town and country, industry and farm and an accompanying text, taken from contemporary writing about Derbyshire, provides the voice of people of the time.

Old photographs have a strong appeal for most of us. By the late nineteenth century photography had become a very popular medium and fortunately there remain large collections of photographs of all subjects from this period for us to study. The collection here has been chosen to provide a broad picture of the county from picturesque views of the dales and moors, that attracted so many of the photographers, to the more socially and historically important scenes of working mills and mines that were less often photographed. Some old photographs can be misleading, quite often professionally taken views were posed or 'ideal' scenes and it is as well to remember that the reality behind some of these pictures of rural contentment may have been rather different from what is suggested. The worn working clothes and weather-beaten face of a subject may tell us more of the real conditions.

It is perhaps surprising to find that by the mid-nineteenth century the Peak District in particular, was already a very popular tourist attraction, at least that is, for those who could afford to travel. Many guides to the area were written at this time, often in the form of 'visitor's tales' and make fascinating reading today. These books necessarily dwell on the beauty of the landscape or the nature of the fishing that was to be enjoyed by the visitor but less often tell of the people of Derbyshire. They have nonetheless been a useful source of material for a view of the county by outsiders but for the residents' view I have looked to biographies and reminiscences of farmers, miners and others to whom Derbyshire was home.

Most of the photographs and written material I have chosen date from the 1880s to just after the turn of the century and although a few fall just outside these limits the latter have been included if I felt that they had something to contribute and remained typical of the period of about a century ago. I have not attempted to include all the towns and villages but there is a wide geographical spread and I hope that I have managed to represent fairly, most areas of the county.

I have added quite short captions to the photographs, sufficient usually, simply to locate the picture but fuller details, including the dates when known, are listed, with the sources of the originals, at the end of the book. There is also a complete source list for the written material; should an extract

TREAK CLIFF CAVERN, CASTLETON

1

LONG BRIDGE, STANTON-BY-BRIDGE

LUKE GARSIDE, HAYFIELD

whet the appetite for a fuller read, it will be possible to trace the original book and do so.

Assembling the material for this book has given me a great deal of pleasure and I hope that the result will give as much pleasure to others. Whilst working on it I have received help from many people who have loaned photographs, books and given me useful research leads, I should like to thank them all. In particular I should like to thank the following: Ray Rippingale and Bob Ball, Derbyshire Library Service; Jean Radford and Ruth Gordon, Matlock Local Studies Library; the staff of Derby Local Studies Library; Maxwell Craven, Derby Museum; Margaret O'Sullivan and the staff of Derbyshire Record Office, Matlock; the staff of the National Railway Museum, York; Michael Pearman, The Library, Chatsworth; Kerry Usher, Calke Abbey; Gill Weston, Melbourne Hall; Brian Thornton, British Coal (Opencast) Archives, Mansfield; Howard Usher, Melbourne Civic Society; Tony Bowker, Masson Mill, Cromford; Gordon Coupe, Youlgrave; Leslie Cox, Twyford; Beryl Edmonds, Matlock; Tony Holmes, Wirksworth; David Roberts, Chesterfield; Sheila Tomlins, Little Eaton; Cliff Williams, Clay Cross, Francis and Pearl Winfield, Matlock.

Finally, thanks to my own family, Sue, Rupert and Tom for their help and patience whilst I was compiling the book and to my parents, Ray and Barbara Buxton, for putting me up so often during my trips aroumd the county.

David Buxton
September 1992

Introduction

Derbyshire is a county packed with natural beauty of great variety from the heights of the Peak District, the nation's first designated National Park, to the valleys of great rivers like the Derwent, the Trent and the Wye. It has fine parks where historic families have lived for centuries, like Chatsworth, Calke and Kedleston, medieval manor houses like Haddon Hall and the now ruinous Wingfield Manor and a good selection of well-preserved village crosses such as those at Bonsall and Repton. It is a county that has attracted visitors to its charms for centuries and although it now attracts more tourists than at any time in its past there are still huge tracts of wild, open space that cannot be reached by the motor car and therefore demand the committment of a long walk from the visitor.

Although it is best known for the beauty of its landscape it was central to some important developments during the Industrial Revolution. Derby was the home of the first silk mill in England, is still the home of one of the nation's oldest and best known china works, Royal Crown Derby and later was the town chosen by Messrs Rolls and Royce to establish a famous car factory. The modern textile industry had its origins in the activities of some late eighteenth-century Derbyshire, industrial pioneers: at Cromford, Richard Arkwright who invented the spinning frame, built the first mill to be operated by water-power and in partnership with Jedidiah Strutt gave the impetus for the development of the cotton industry and a factory system for mass production. Arkwright's Masson Mill built in 1784, also at Cromford, saw

LOVERS' WALK, MATLOCK BATH

3

the continuous manufacture of cotton thread until its final closure in October 1991.

The north east of the county has seen the longest industrial interest of all since the Romans discovered and mined the lead ore in the hills of this region. Some of the mines were in continuous use from the time of the Romans until earlier this century. The eastern border of the county has for at least two centuries been the coalmining belt of the area bringing prosperity to its mine-owners, if not to the miners, until the enforced decline of that industry in Britain in the last decade.

Farming in the county is dictated by the terrain of the regions, thus the lusher areas of the south and south west, the valleys of the Trent and Dove, have traditionally been dairying areas, so productive in the past that one town, Ashbourne, became a centre for the factory processing of dairy products. At Twyford on the river Trent, a dairy farmer who lived in the village and over-wintered his cattle in the farmyard, took his herd to summer pasture on the other side of the river which is wide at this point. To reach the pasture it was necessary to first walk the cattle several miles to the nearest bridge and back again. Twice a day, all summer, the farmer crossed the river by ferry (p. 83) to milk the cows in the field and then return with the full milk-cans on the boat. At the end of summer the herd returned to the shelter of the farm via the distant bridge.

In the north and the Peak Park there is less land available for this sort of farming and the high altitude and harsher winters make it a terrain more suited to sheep than cows, although some arable and dairying is done. There are some first-hand accounts of farming near the village of Sheldon (over 1000 ft) at the turn of the century, including detailed accounts of the traditional ways of cutting and stacking oats and wheat in this area.

CHESTERFIELD

The late Victorian period was one of hardship for many sections of the community. It was a time of economic upheaval and many were materially worse off than the two generations before them. In farming there had been serious set-backs, some of which began with the repeal of the Corn Laws in 1846. Protection of wheat prices from foreign competition had preserved the income of farmers in the first half of the century, although it was not obvious that their labourers had benefitted very much, but a gradual fall in wheat prices in the second half, coupled with a succession of poor harvests, had sealed the fate of many farmers by the 1880s. Farms in the south of England, who depended far more on wheat crops suffered the most but a general depression in farming occurred throughout the land.

Farm labourers were not the only disadvantaged groups and tales of hardship resulting from hard work and low pay are common throughout industrial, Victorian England. It was an irony that whilst the rise of the factory society provided much needed employment and income, drawing people into the towns, it produced levels of exploitation previously unimagined in rural experience. The textile mills of the Midlands and North provided work but at an enormous human cost; whole families, including small children, worked most of their waking hours in monotonous and often dangerous work for small wages. The lack of effective workers organisations here and in other workplaces allowed employers to hold workers to ransom. The coal industry was also notorious in this respect. In 1893 mine-owners announced a cut in wages of 25%, affecting 300,000 miners across the country. Most miners refused to accept this cut in their already meagre earnings and pit 'lockouts' were imposed that lasted for four and a half months. The hardship was severe for the mining families and relief organisations were set up. At Clay Cross one such committee provided a total of 45,000 meals and the town's allotment society distributed vegetables to the 'locked-out' men and their families but the sacrifices were to no avail, they eventually returned to work accepting the new rates. First-hand accounts of these times are recalled by a Derbyshire miner in this book and there are photographs too of miners during the 'lock-out', coal-picking for fuel on the waste-heaps (p. 76). Some pictures of miners at work include one of boy miners so young they could hardly reach the safety bar of the descent platform taking them down the pit (p. 38).

It is difficult to imagine a greater contrast in lifestyles than that which was experienced by the workers in the pits and mills of the late Victorian era and those of their near neighbours who owned the great country estates. At nearby houses like Chatsworth and Kedleston a privileged minority lived in fabulous luxury, building lavish houses and gardens, collecting works of art and entertaining royalty. The gardens at Chatsworth were rated second only to those at Windsor for their beauty and size. It was here that Joseph Paxton had transformed the gardens for the sixth Duke of Devonshire and built new glasshouses that were the prototype for his crowning glory, the great Crystal Palace in London in 1851. The Duke employed a workforce of eighty gardeners in 1900. The gar-

ASHBOURNE CARD PLAYERS

delights the eye and impresses the imagination far beyond the power of the words to describe.

Although a visitor to the area he recorded not only his opinions on the scenery but also relates conversations he had with people he met on the way: farmers, gipsies, tinkers and commercial travellers all receive space in his accounts.

Not all visitors to Derbyshire at this time came for walking tours or fishing in the river Dove. Many came to take the 'treatments' at Buxton or Matlock. The warm, mineral waters at Buxton had first attracted the Romans to the area and centuries later the fashionable infirm were still visiting the town to bathe in or drink the waters. Buxton's heyday as a spa town was in the late eighteenth and nineteenth centuries and many of the town's buildings date from the late Georgian period reflecting the demand for hotel accommodation, hospitals, thermal baths and treatment centres. The magnificent Crescent, modelled on the larger one at Bath, and the Devonshire Hospital with its enormous domed roof, the largest span in the world at the time, were both built by the Dukes of Devonshire. At Matlock, however, where there had also been a long asscociation with 'spa treatments', the style of treatment underwent a change that set Matlock apart from other towns like Buxton. In the 1850s, a wealthy Matlock hosier, John Smedley who had suffered a prolonged illness following a trip abroad, sought relief from his complaint in 'hydropathic treatment'. The treatment he received, a weird combination of hot and cold baths, mustard packs and steam was followed, several months later, by recovery from the illness. Smedley attributed his recovery to the treatment he had received and so impressed with it was he that he purchased a house in Matlock where he proposed to treat the people of Matlock himself. Totally without medical experience he ventured, initially, to offer, hydropathic treatment for his own employees who fell sick but the success of his efforts led him to expand his operations to provide treatment for first, the poor of Matlock and later for anyone who sought it and could pay.

den devoted five acres to fruit growing, three acres to vegetables and a further two to flowers for bedding plants. There were no less than thirty glasshouses including the colossal Great Conservatory (p. 62) and the so-called Victoria Regia house (p. 63), three orchid houses, four pineapple houses, three ranges of vineries (250 ft long), a mushroom house, cucumber and melon houses, several peach houses, strawberry and cherry houses, the Orangery and several others. The gardens and house were open to the public and to all accounts attracted large numbers of visitors. It is interesting to note from this account written in 1880 that the tourists then were no more respectful than some of their counterparts today:

> It cannot be said that the Duke of Devonshire is niggardly towards the public, nor are they wanting in generosity towards him in return, for before going away they invariably make a present of all their sandwich-papers and empty bottles, and carefully place them where there is no danger of their being overlooked.

This sarcastic observation on the habits of the Victorian tourist was made by Louis J. Jennings in his excellent book *Rambles Among the Hills* in which he describes, in some detail, most corners of the Peak and also something of its inhabitants. These are the views of a leisured gentleman on a walking holiday. A great lover of the unspoilt countryside he hated the commercialisation of the more popular areas, particularly Matlock Bath, and was highly intolerant of crowds and 'trippers'. He believed the famous 'beauty spot', Dove Dale, overrated and the fashionable spa town, Buxton, 'not a place which the traveller or sketcher will desire to visit more than once'. He was happiest when out of the well-trodden areas, as on a walk alone up Kinder Scout:

> ... over a bridge across a mountain torrent, through most charming scenery, the glorious hills extending far and wide all covered with heath in full bloom ... which

THE TERRACE AT SMEDLEY'S HYDRO

Interest in his treatment grew so rapidly that by the 1860s he had completed the building of an enormous edifice on the hill at Matlock Bank to accommodate the demand. Smedley's Hydro, as it became known, not only housed treatment baths and facilities but also hotel-style accommodation for the visitors with gardens, tennis courts and a ballroom for evening entertainments. Although the accommodation and communal dining arrangements were simple rather than lavish, a visit to the 'hydro' soon became a fashionable thing to include in the round of social activities for some members of the Victorian and Edwardian middle-classes. Smedley's success encouraged others to open similar establishments and by the turn of the century Matlock had a collection of 'hydros', each, it was noticeable, promoting their leisure attractions as well as water treatments. The 'hydros' remained popular in Matlock until the late 1930s when the Second World War brought enforced closure. Smedley's Hydro was appropriated by the Ministry of Health at the outbreak of war and although it re-opened afterwards it never regained its previous popularity.

For some of the examples of Derbyshire farming life of the period I have drawn on the books of Alison Uttley who was a farmer's daughter at Castle Top Farm near Cromford. She is well-known to generations of children for her stories of *Little Grey Rabbit* but she also wrote some memorable books about her own childhood too. These reminiscences of life in rural Derbyshire around the turn of the century bring cheerfully to life a child's view of farming, seasonal celebrations, traditional foods, first schooldays and even memories of bath-time by the fire. These beautifully written pieces, in romantic style, succeed in bringing to life all the characters of her childhood; her parents, the farmhands, village shopkeepers and even her schoolmistress. By a lucky chance, I also came across a photograph of the schoolmistress in an album so we can actualy see what she looked like. She is sitting in the front row of a group

MR SEAMAN THE PHOTOGRAPHER

photograph of the Derbyshire Entomological Society on an excursion in 1890 (p. 68).

What of the photographers who took the views that appear in the book? Unfortunately many of them must remain unknown because their names have long since been separated from their photographs, but a little is known about some of them. A Norwegian photographer, Hans Hansen, came to Ashbourne and in about 1890 married a daughter of the Haycock family of Ashbourne clockmakers, and set up a photographic studio. A self-portrait of Hansen (obviously a man with a sense of humour) can be seen on the title page and his wife and daughter opposite. Several more of his excellent photographs from in and around Ashbourne taken from his stereoscopic slides, are included in the book.

A name that often occurs on photographs of the period is that of Seaman and Sons. The firm had studios in several Derbyshire towns including Chesterfield and Ilkeston but the main one was probably in Temple Road, Matlock Bath. Mr Seaman is seen (below) here taking a photograph of himself with his stereo-camera in a wall-mirror at Smedley's Hydro, following a commission to photograph the establishment and its staff. The firm had a shop in Chesterfield until quite recently.

In the south of the county a well-known name in photography was that of Edward Martin who lived and had a studio in Ashby Road, Melbourne from about 1890 until the 1920s. He was a familiar figure around Melbourne on his bicycle with a special basket on the front to hold the photographic equipment. A large number of his glass negatives were discovered recently and some prints from these have been used. Like many photographers he often commandeered local children to pose for his views but Martin went to greater lengths than most in using them to give his pictures more interest value (p. 80).

No book containing old photographs of Derbyshire would be complete without some examples of the work of Richard Keene of Derby. Keene was a pioneer photographer in the town and worked from a studio in Irongate from the early 1850s until his death in 1894. He was a prolific photographer and won prizes for his photographs. As well as recording the changing scenes of Derby's streets in the second half of the last century, some of which are reproduced here, he also recorded picturesque views of the county which he offered for sale as in this advertisement of 1892;

Photographs of Derby and Derbyshire
R. Keene begs to inform the public that he has
ready for sale upwards of 3,000 views
of the beautiful and interesting
scenery, antiquities, churches, halls, ruins, etc.,
of the County of Derbyshire

Now, having looked briefly at the historical background to the setting of the book and been introduced to some of the many writers and photographers whose work forms the source material, I hope that you will go on to enjoy this new and modern presentation of their work, providing, as it does, a glimpse of *Derbyshire of one hundred years ago.*

DERBYSHIRE

of one hundred years ago

Church & Turret Clocks

AND
CARILLON MACHINERY
MADE BY

JOHN SMITH & SONS,

Midland Clock Works,

QUEEN STREET,
DERBY.
ENGLAND.

SPEEDWELL CAVERN AND WINNATS PASS, CASTLETON

CAVERNS

The Speedwell Mine is distant about half-a-mile from Castleton, on the left of the old Buxton Road, and close to the entrance to the Winnats. It was originally excavated by a company of proprietors in search of lead ore, but the result proved unfortunate; and, after eleven years' fruitless toil, and an expenditure of £14,000, it was finally abandoned, the principal shareholder, a Mr Oakden, of Staffordshire, having been ruined by the undertaking. It now remains only an object of attraction to the curious, and a monument of mining skill and patient industry unhappily unrewarded.

The entrance is mean and unpretending, in this respect contrasting unfavourably with the magnificent approach to Peak's Hole – a low white-washed cottage, with the name painted over the door, being the only outward indication of its existence.

Descending by a flight of upwards of a hundred steps, we arrived at a 'level,' or subterranean canal, some six or seven feet in breadth, that has been hewn out of the limestone, where we found a long narrow boat, capable of seating about twenty persons, in readiness, in which we embarked, the guide impelling us along by pushing against the sides of the rock. There was just sufficient room to sit upright in the boat without knocking our heads against the top, the channel

being not more than eight or nine feet from the roof to the bottom of the water – the latter being about three or four feet in depth. At the commencement of the journey our conductor placed a lighted candle against the side, and others again at short intervals as we went along, and so straight is the excavation that, looking back, they could be distinctly seen the entire length – the reflection upon the still water presenting, as may readily be imagined, a very pleasing effect. As the boat glides along, several veins of lead ore are seen, though none sufficiently rich to repay the cost of working. In places sudden breaks and fissures appear at right angles with the passage that look as if nature had begun a series of transepts, and then abandoned the design; and here and there huge rents are seen, caused by the cooling of the vast limestone mass in primeval days. Then we come to the Half-way House, where a tunnel branches off to the right. For a time the stillness was almost unearthly, then the echoes were awoke by our companion playing Luther's grand old hymn upon the bugle, the tones reverberating back through the long watery vault, producing an effect that will leave an echo in the memory to life's latest day. As the sounds died away we became conscious of a hollow murmuring in the distance, the sound of which increased as we proceeded on until it became a loud roar, caused as we learned by the water falling into the 'Bottomless Pit.'

CASTLETON

We had traversed a distance of seven hundred and fifty yards and had now reached the Grand Cavern, a vast opening fashioned by nature in the heart of the mountain, the height and depth of which have never yet been ascertained. Huge bulging masses of rock stand out on either hand as if they were about to topple down upon us, and everywhere the roof and sides are intersected by fissures that have been either formed or enlarged by the erosive action of water passing through them for successive ages. Across the opening a broad archway or platform, protected by an iron railing, has been erected for the accommodation of visitors. Mooring our boat to the rock, we ascended this, the better to survey the abyss beneath; and strange indeed must be the feeling, and firm the resolution, of the man who could stand upon this spot and look down into the unfathomable gulf in which the seething waters plunge night and day into the deep darkness, without experiencing a sensation of the profoundest awe. As we leaned over the railing and gazed into the immense void, the feeble and sickly light of our candles, overpowered by the impervious gloom, whilst they failed to illuminate, served to render the surrounding darkness still more striking and apparent. Miners have been let down this chasm a distance of ninety feet, at which point commences a pool of water that is said to have swallowed up 40,000 tons of rubbish, produced in driving the level from 600 to 700 yards beyond the cavern, without making any perceptible difference either in extent or depth. The so-called pool is,

however, nothing more than an underground current communicating with other caverns, along which the rubbish has no doubt been carried by the force of the stream.

The height of the dome has never been determined, but the distance to the surface of the mountain has been computed at eight hundred and forty feet, and nearly the whole of the intervening space is believed to be one vast cavity. We peered into the darkness, but our candles were too feeble to illuminate the lofty roof, and the gloom was more palpable from the absence of ornament – no gleaming stalactites or glittering crystallisations giving back the dim candle flame. Steps have been formed by placing wooden pegs across a cleft in the rocks for a considerable way upwards, and up these the guide climbed and fired a blue-light which revealed to us for a few moments some of the hidden recesses of this magnificent cavern, but there was still a space above which the light failed to penetrate. Some idea of the altitude of this cavern may be formed from the fact that rockets of sufficient strength to ascend 450 feet have been discharged, and have risen unimpeded to their highest elevation, exploded, and thrown out their brilliant coruscations as freely as if they had ascended beneath the vault of heaven.

The visitor is generally entertained with a 'blast' before leaving the cavern, for which a trifling additional charge is made. A small quantity of gunpowder is wedged in the rock and fired, the sound of the explosion reverberating from side to side with fearful intonation.

PEACOCK HOTEL, BASLOW

Having completed our examination of the Speedwell Mine, we lost no time in visiting the Blue John Cavern, another, and certainly not the least interesting of the Derbyshire wonders. This cavern is situated near the foot of Tray Cliff, immediately opposite the shivering front of Mam Tor. By the carriage road it is distant about a mile and a half from Castleton; but pedestrians will find a much shorter route by following a narrow track that leads across the edge of the cliff.

This cavern is the grand depository of the amethystine or topazine fluor of mineralogists, locally designated Blue John.

Descending by a flight of steps we reached a narrow confined passage that winds between stupendous rocks which appear to have been rent asunder by some convulsive effort of nature. From the roof of this passage stalactites are pendant, and all along, the sides are coated with crystals of carbonate of lime, and embedded with fossil shells, entrochi, coralloids, madrepores, and a host of others that have not seen the light since these rocks were deposited as calcareous mud upon the bottoms of the carboniferous seas. In some places huge masses of detached rock project into the pathway, threatening a barrier to all further progress; in others the limestone is dislocated and broken into a diversity of forms, rugged as chaos, then the pathway gets rougher, and we go twining between damp slimy walls of rock, and a little further on we come to a crystalline

SPEEDWELL CAVERN

VIA GELLA

spring in a hollow on the left, so transparent as to be treacherous in the certain light. After proceeding some distance a spacious opening is reached one hundred and fifty feet in height and about sixty feet in diameter, called Lord Mulgrave's Dining-room, from the circumstance of its having been used as such by the Marquis of Normanby and the miners who accompanied him on his three days' subterranean expedition in the endeavour to discover another outlet.

James Croston

Bacon or Rabbit?

Presently I came to a horse hobbled, grazing on the grass which fringed the road. A little further on was a pot hanging on three sticks over a wood fire, and near it were seated a dark woman and a little child. The woman looked at me as I suddenly appeared above the hedge, and muttered a few words, in reply to which a man came out from a thicket and stood staring hard. The dark woman's eyes shone in the fire light like big black beads.

'Good evening,' said I.

'Good evening,' said the man, concealing something in one hand behind him, and looking very distrustfully upon me.

'I see how it is,' said I; 'you take me for a keeper. But if nobody intereferes more than I shall do with what you have got cooking in the pot there, your supper will be safe enough. It smells good.'

'There is nothing but a bit of bacon in there and a few potatoes,' said the man; 'no harm in that, is there?'

'Not the least in life – any more than there will be in your washing it down with some ale,' and I handed over a trifle for that purpose. This at once smoothed the ground, for keepers are not in the habit of giving beer-money to gipsies.

'Your wife, I see, comes from the true old stock.'

'She does, sir,' said the man; 'she is one of the Lees, and a clever woman too – aren't you, Nance?'

The dark woman smiled, and smoothed out her black hair with her hand, and drew her child closer to her, for the air was chilly. It was so dark that I had not at first noticed their little house on wheels.

'What luck to be in the open air all day, and carry your house round with you!' said I. 'Will you take it amiss if I ask to see the inside of it?'

The man hesitated and looked at his wife, but she giving no sign of opposition, he lit a candle in an old lantern, and took me up the steps, and I followed him. The first compartment was filled with crockery and odds and ends, and the second was a small but not uncomfortable place, about the size of a cabin on board ship, with a bed and few articles of furniture in it, and with neat curtains at each window, tied up in the mid-

MASSON MILL, CROMFORD

dle with a bit of blue ribbon. Altogether, it was as snug a place as any man could wish for – one could be as happy there as in a palace.

'I would rather live here and go where I liked than have a house in Belgrave Square,' said I.

'Perhaps you would, sir, in summer,' replied the man; 'but when the rain and snow came you would tell a different story. Especially if you had gone all day without making a copper, or having anything to eat. Last winter we knew what that was more than once, for you see, sir, it was a hard winter, with lots of snow. You could scarcely get along this road, and yet this is about the best road we travel.'

'Does your wife tell fortunes?'

'She does not, sir, for if she did the peelers would be after us. But she knows all about it – perhaps she would not mind telling you yours on the quiet.'

'Thank you, but mine would puzzle her too much.' We came down the steps again and out into the air. 'I hope you will enjoy your rabbit – I mean your bacon,' said I to the man as I wished him good night.

I left him with a queer smile on his face, and presently the fire shrank to the dimensions of a red-hot coal, and then disappeared altogether in the distance.

Louis J. Jennings

TRADE OUTRAGE: RATTENING AT COOK'S MILL

Between the hours of twelve and one o'clock on Wednesday, at Messrs R. Cook and Co's, hackle-pin manufacturers Hathersage, some evilly disposed person or persons maliciously placed a brick between two cog wheels in a shop known as the 'scouring shop'. The dastardly deed was discovered as soon as the engine (which is a powerful one) commenced to run, and a loud report was heard, and on examination it was found the shaft had been broken. A similar attempt was made two or three weeks ago in a different part of the mill to do damage to some of the machinery, but fortunately it was found out in time. The offender is evidently someone who knows the 'runs' of the works, as not a trace of the act can be brought to reflect upon anyone at present. The workmen had all gone to dinner. The accident has caused a stoppage to part of the works.

High Peak News, 11 January 1890

HOW I BECAME A POACHER

Old Mr Sharpe told these stories of his life during the evenings. We used to sit one on each side of the fireplace. Mr

TWO DALES

Sharpe would lean back in his easy chair, shading his eyes as he questioned, 'What are we on with tonight?'

'Just what you like,' I used to reply obligingly.

One day he said, 'Aye, well, how would it be if we do, 'How and why I became a poacher'? That would be a good title, wouldn't it?'

I agreed that it would and Sharpy continued in a voice at once wistful and proud as he said, 'You know I've never been a child, I've *always* been a man.' (It was the prelude to this story.)

It was a beautiful night towards the latter end of corn harvest. The peace of fulfillment lay over the whole countryside; the golden rays of a westering sun bathing every object with shimmering light. We were all out of doors. Men and women, boys and girls, we stood in a group quietly talking or just admiring the peaceful splendour of the earth.

Suddenly a gun went off! It shattered instantly that atmosphere of deep content. It startled us and we all looked in the direction from which we heard the shot. We saw four men and a dog. As we looked we saw that they were fighting. It looked like a scrap between keepers and a poacher and so it proved to be.

The keepers having set the dog after the poacher, it got hold of his clothes. The keepers shouted it back, but seeing that the poacher was getting away they set the dog on him again. When he saw the dog was coming back he shot the dog and some of the shot hit a keeper. Thereafter the poacher's fate was sealed.

With vengeance in their hearts, the keepers caught up with the man who had defied them. They grabbed his gun and took it to pieces and then they thrashed him with it. Aye, there was nothing soft about them, they thrashed him all right. I remember the indignation amongst the watchers and my mother jumping from the wall on which she had been sitting and exclaiming angrily, 'I'm not sitting by and watching that!'

With furious determination showing in every movement she hurried to the spot where the struggle still went on. There she found that the poacher was her brother! My mother's intervention stopped the thrashing but my uncle was arrested and was later sentenced to four months imprisonment. Witnessing this beating roused my blood till I would have done anything against the keepers. I determined to be a poacher myself. For a long time I kept my word.

Old Mr Sharpe's voice fell into silence and I ventured to make an enquiry.

'How old were you then?'

'Twelve,' Sharpy replied, his chin sinking on his breast and looking at me with quizzical eyes. 'You see,' he went on patiently, 'I've always been a man.'

The accent was on the word 'always'. His voice was wistful as well as proud.

'Ever seen a snickle?' The gamin smile peeped out, while I had to confess my ignorance; such crass ignorance! Slowly and deliberately Sharpy explained.

While my uncle was in prison most of my spare time was spent making snickles. A snickle is a rabbit snare. Aye, I've

SHELDON SCHOOL

made many a hundred. We used to make them out of pop bottle wires. I remember the first time I set the snickles I caught a rabbit and from then on I was always a poacher. Once a poacher, the lure of the fields at night is well nigh irresistible, quite apart from the material profit of the ventures, which can be considerable. My uncle too had poaching in the blood. No sooner was he released from prison than he was up to his old tricks again. One summer day, he had been setting snickles and in one he had captured a hare but didn't dare collect it, for he knew that three keepers were lying in wait for him, hidden in a dyke about twenty yards off, by a hedge that separated two fields. With superb indifference my uncle walked past the keepers empty handed. It was sheer impudence when you think of it considering the plan he had in mind, though he may have been more than a little apprehensive. When he arrived home, he became full of a cool urgency.

'Now, Martha,' he instructed my mother, 'there's a hare in a snickle about twenty yards from the lane bottom, along that hedge, and twenty yards further on there's keepers hidden in a dyke. If you go blackberrying I'll put thee a belt on and I'll put thee this hook on and this piece of band with a slip noose.

Put a loose frock on, slip this round t'hare's neck and hang it on this hook and drop thee frock.' Such were his orders and my mother agreed to go. I remember it as clear as if it was yesterday, walking down a lane and while we were apparently blackberrying, my mother accomplished her errand. Under the very noses of the keepers she took the hare and walked home with it under her frock. Later it chanced that my uncle met one of the keepers in the street. They greeted each other seemingly as friends and the keeper conceded, 'You've overmanned us this time, Hawkins.'

Nellie Connole

SHELDON CHILDHOOD

I can remember that Saturday night was bath night. This was in a zinc bath on the hearth in front of the fire. Mother would very often be making pastry for the week-end or baking, keeping an eye on us children at the same time. I remember

THE MORLEDGE, DERBY

OCKBROOK

once when she had just pulled a jam pasty from the oven, I must stand up and put my fingers in it as it was on the corner of the table. Of course I let out a yell, as there is nothing much hotter than jam, and mother grabbed my fingers and licked the jam off.

Our butcher always came on Saturday night, usually as we were having a bath. He would knock, open the door, and shout 'Roast, toast, boil or fry, frizzle, stew or bake, anything tonight, mam?' Of course, on a cold, frosty night it made a terrible draught, and mother would tell him to shut the door and she would attend to him in a minute. Night work was a very common thing then. The grocer came on a Wednesday night, anything up to 9.30, and would stop, talking at most of his calls. His poor old horse stood with its cover on, now and again with a nose-bag of corn, patiently waiting for its master to go home. The greengrocer also used to get home at all hours, usually turning the horse out to grass in summer at midnight or later.

We used to take turns telling fairy tales when we went to bed, then if mother heard us she would call up to tell us to go to sleep. We would then say 'Tell father to play something', and he would usually get his concertina out and we would soon be asleep.

F.W. Brocklehurst

BONNETS AND PINAFORES

In memory I see people towering above me, giants, just as they must have looked to me as a child, and their clothes have all the strangeness they had for me when I was under six. I am pressed against full striped skirts, with silver-buckled belts and pockets hidden in many folds at the back, or held to stout bosoms encased in hard whalebone stays. Bosoms alarmed me, especially the high-breasted kind. I preferred people to be flat, like my mother, without any protuberances, although, on the whole, I liked fat people better than thin ones. There was bead-trimming down many of these bosoms, which scratched my cheeks, or braid, in whorls and curls, twisting in fascinating spirals. The bodices had buttons of cut steel, or bright jet, or barrel-shaped braid buttons, but under this array was a row of hooks and eyes which fastened the lining, with its bones and stiffening.

Behind my mother's bedroom door and in her wardrobe were her dresses, of grey cashmere, of black silk, and of plum-coloured merino, with acorn-shaped buttons and silk buttons, with frills and ribbons and lace tuckers. There was a sweet scent about the clothes which I loved, and often I buried my face in the folds and sniffed for five minutes, breathing in the

TEA AT LATHKILL DALE

odour of some fragrant herb. I was sent to feel in the pocket for a lost handkerchief, or a purse, or keys, for pockets were so large they held a goodly number of things, but although I could feel the bulk of the pocket, I could not find my way in through the crowded pleats, and I struggled, standing on a chair to reach with my fingers impatiently trying to discover the hole. Sometimes I gave it up, and went downstairs without the object, only to be sent back for another attempt. The way a grown-up's pocket was concealed was always a mystery to me, for my own pocket was very conspicuous.

In summer my mother wore creamy holland dresses piped with white linen. Lizzie Wildgoose came from an upland cottage to stay for a week, to do the dress-making, and help with mending. My own little frocks were made from the same lengths of holland, with turned down collars and full sleeves. My brother and I wore holland garibaldis one summer, and we were very proud to hear they were named after a soldier. The name was a fine-sounding one, and I always said it with gusto, shouting 'Garibaldi! Garibaldi!' when my clean starched blouse with its square collar came out of the linen drawer.

Over my dress I always wore a pinafore, of white starched linen, with lace frills round the neck and armholes. Pinafores and sashes were the most important articles of my apparel. The

pinafore kept the dress clean, the sash adorned it. Every morning I put on a fresh pinafore, and I tried to keep it spotless, but at night it was soiled. On Sundays I had fine diaper pinafores with lace insertion, inherited from richer folk.

My dresses had rows of tucks, seven or eight, and as I grew they were taken out, so that the dress kept pace with me. It was a shameful thing to have a dress too short. The Sunday dress which I remember best, for I was photographed in it when I was five, was a honeycombed terracotta cashmere, with bishop sleeves, which crept higher and higher up my arms as I grew taller. It had so many tucks I wore it for years, its fullness kept in place by a wide red silk sash.

I wore fringed silk sashes on Sundays, over my loose dresses, and waistbands of starched holland on weekdays. There was an immense blue and white silk sash, half a yard broad, which was my best, a salmon silk for birthdays and tea-parties, and an Indian one for driving out. The sashes were put on with great care by my mother, fold after fold arranged round my waist in a pleated effect, and then a great bow was tied at my back, and I was set free from the long wait.

When I was three and a half I went to church wearing a red velvet bonnet and a caped coat. The bonnet was tall, with a stiff oval back, and a pleated crown, with a frill of red and

BIRCHWOOD CHAPEL, RIDDINGS

white silk inside next to my cheeks. I remember the warmth of it over my ears and the shut-in feeling when the ribbons were tied under my chin. This bonnet was so much loved by my mother that she kept it for years. Whenever I opened a certain drawer I found my bonnet lying there, and I marvelled at its colour and richness. Other bonnets followed this, fawn and brown with beaver edgings.

Lastly, I had a grey cloak lined with scarlet and edged with fur, which was made by my mother and Lizzie. With it I wore a grey hood, also fur-bordered. It was a copy of Red Riding-hood's own head-dress, and was reversible, so that I was either in scarlet or grey. I was smothered in its thick folds, and I was aware that no one at church wore a hood like mine. We did not follow the fashions, we made our own styles, but my father was ashamed to be seen driving his pony and trap with a big girl of six in a bonnet beside him. His ridicule helped me to escape from the bondage of bonnets.

Sunbonnets, of course, were the summer wear for the fields and country journeys, and I had finely ruffled and pleated buff and pale pink bonnets, tied under my chin. For school I wore a round sailor hat with a blue ribbon dangling down the back.

When I had finished with bonnets I wore a Leghorn straw hat on Sundays in summer, and a 'real beaver' with little pom-poms on the side in winter. These hats served me for years, for 'very best', and I had a real affection for them. When I was seven or thereabouts, I read a moral little story of a girl who grumbled at her clothes.

'Last year's hat!' she cried.

MR BAGSHAW, MATLOCK

LOSCOE GRANGE

I couldn't understand this tale, for I loved last year's hat, with its dear familiar smell, its comfortable shape, adapted to my head, its bitter elastic. The elastic particularly enamoured me, and the narrow band under each hat had its own characteristics. I knew where it was smooth, where it was knobby with frayed edges, and the knot in the middle, where it had been tightened, was a friend. Elastic under the chin was a solace to a lonely child, like the touch of a beloved hand on one's face. It was food on a long walk when pangs of hunger assailed me, and I nibbled and sucked the elastic under my everyday hat as I walked the miles to school. I held it with one finger when I was frightened, to give myself confidence, and, when I was happy and carefree, I swung my hat by it, or let the shady straw hang down my back, held to my neck by the loop.

Unfortunately my mother didn't like my bitten tangled elastics, and every few weeks she insisted on putting in a fresh one. After the first few hours of strangeness, I made overtures to it, and once more I had a companion.

Every Sunday, when I took off my Leghorn hat, I was told to stuff the pink bows with tissue paper to keep them upright, before I put it away in its box. My beaver hat was wrapped in a large handkerchief before it was placed in the hat drawer. It was necessary to take great care of one's Sunday clothes.

My clothes were plain and few, from the white chemise which I wore next to my skin, to the top layer of frock and pinafore, and everything was home-made except the Liberty bodice on which my stockings were fastened. Buttoned to the bodice were white drawers with Torchon lace around the edges. I was proud of my drawers, garments which must never be seen or the disgrace was terrible, but I remember comparing the lace edges with those of another little girl at school, lifting my skirt and showing my finery with a desperate boldness as I tried to impress her. Under my frock was a white petticoat in summer and a hand-crocheted scarlet one in winter.

I needed all the warmth I could get, for I went to school in all weathers, walking through snowstorms and torrents of rain, thunder and lightning. Soon my clothes were wet through, I had no mackintosh, nor did I ever see one among the children. My little umbrella was often swept from my grasp, and turned inside out, an occurrence which filled me with chagrin, for boys laughed as I struggled with the broken ribs and torn cover. I could not manage an umbrella, and I preferred to go without. I arrived at school or at home, wet to the skin, but happy and warm with my struggle against wind and rain.

My capes and cloaks were my comfort, and I wrapped them tightly around me, and bent my head, on which was perched a

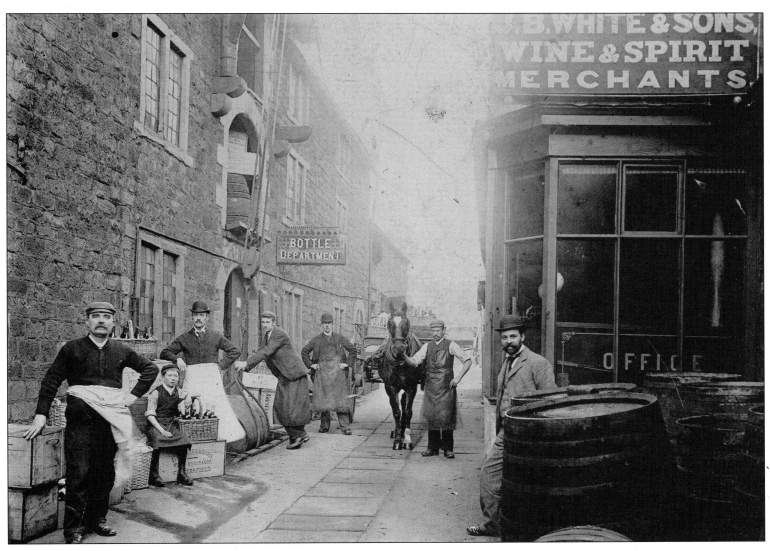

CHESTERFIELD

tam-o'-shanter or a round tweed hat to match my cloak. Then the wind could blow and the rain pour. I went to the schoolmaster's house and took off my wet dress, and sat by the fire draped in somebody's dressing-gown whilst my clothes dried, thankful to miss lessons for a time. At the mature age of six I returned home from a visit to a relation wearing a 'bustle' under my dress. It was a black cushion, heart-shaped, hard as iron, tied round my waist with two long tapes. The bustle made the back project in the absurd town fashion, which had never penetrated to our own simple countryside. When my mother saw me wearing this atrocity she quickly untied it and threw it in the fire, to my satisfaction, for I was afraid to remove it myself.

Alison Uttley

CHESTERFIELD 'COMMERCIALS'

The approaches to Chesterfield will effectually unloose the stoutest grip of legend or fable. The crooked spire, the mean,

dirty shops, the still dirtier-looking people in the streets, the rambling half dilapidated-looking inn opposite the market-place, speedily brought me back to the every-day world. There is something very depressing about the look of Chesterfield; I would have given a great deal to have gone on somewhere else, but it was too late. It was necessary to make the best of it. I asked for the coffee room at the inn, and was told there was none. 'You can go in with the commercial gents,' said a girl. I had always imagined that this room was forbidden ground to anybody and everybody but a commercial traveller. But thither I was sent, and I always do everything I am told when travelling, and pay what I am asked. Consequently, I soon found myself seated before a longish table, with a huge piece of boiled beef, a perfect mountain, at one end, and a joint of roast beef on a smaller scale at the other. There were also a ham, some cold mutton, a pie, and other things, all serving to show how good and pleasant a thing it is to be a commercial traveller. The company present were by no means unmindful of the opportunity before them. One commercial gent with red whiskers helped himself five times, and walked out of the room as if nothing had happened. Another made even that mass of boiled beef look perceptibly less, and swallowed pie-crust as fast as a

GLOSSOP FIRE BRIGADE

street magician bolts his strips of coloured paper. Every gent as he entered the room called for a pair of slippers, of which there seemed to be an endless supply in a cupboard – slippers which have done duty on all sorts of feet, and are still in great favour with the customers of the 'Angel'. The 'Boots' came and put them on – an operation which I thought might have been better performed in a bedroom. The feet of these bagmen were not exactly like 'white mice peeping in and out,' but they showed them to each other and to me quite freely. Having appeased their hunger, they sat down at the tables and wrote in little books, checking off the day's orders or receipts. No one spoke to me except a sharp-looking man, who remarked upon the unwonted size of a mutton chop which I had ordered – it resembled a small saddle – saying, 'It's like a Barnsley chop. I'll have one for breakfast to-morrow.' It was the man who had devoured the pie. Though gorged like an anaconda, he could still let his thoughts dwell sweetly on next morning's breakfast.

All this time I noticed that an elderly and saturnine-looking commercial gent had never taken his eyes off me since I had been in the room. He sat in a corner where he could command me at his ease, and there he transfixed me with his basilisk glance. I thought of offering him a pound or two off my immense mutton chop, but was not sufficiently acquainted with the etiquette of the sacred place to venture to say a word.

By and by the travellers disappeared one by one, and the black-visaged man and I were left alone. Then he took his feet off the horse-hair sofa and came slowly and mysteriously towards me. If he had worn ruffles I should have taken him for a spectre from Bolsover Castle.

'Isn't your name Henderson?' said he, when he got close to me. 'I met you the other day at – what's the name of the place?'

'I wasn't there,' said I, trying to include everything in one comprehensive answer.

'Well, that's strange. Taken any orders here?'

'None at all.'

'What, not taken one?'

'Well, that's bad. Business is all going to the deuce, here, but I should have thought you could have got an order or two. *What* did you say you are travelling in?'

'I am travelling,' said I, as I rose up to leave the room, 'in Notions.'

'In Notions!' he repeated with astonishment; 'what people call Yankee notions?'

I placed my finger upon my lips, and nodded twice and shook my head once, and left the saturnine man to make what he could of it.

Louis J. Jennings

WHATSTANDWELL

FUNERALS AND WEDDINGS

Oh, how those people loved a funeral; next to a wedding, it was jam. I once went to what I called a typical funeral. This was the style: We all stood round the room, with solemn elongated faces; the usual finger biscuits with British Port and Sherry were silently handed round. Then came the gloves. The Undertaker said, in stentorian tones, 'The company will now view the corpse.' Then the sad procession round the parlour table began. When all had taken their last look at the 'dear departed', in this case an old man, whose relations are longing to hear the will, we returned to the room we had been refreshed in. Once again our undertaker cried, 'handkerchiefs out, all! Ready!' Great excitement prevailed in the lane as we poured out. Happily we only had a few yards to go to the cemetery, and I had to go on first to put on my surplice. We returned to tea; the awful solemnity began to give way, and by the time tea was over, thanks to the quality and quantity of 'brown cream' in the tea, the feast became quite jovial. I doubt if the poor old man has ever had a passing thought since.

A wedding feast at that time of day had so many low and disgusting features that it baffles all possible description. Such things could not happen now, as I have seen happen there and then. I have often heard Killamarsh called bad names, but never had I seen or heard anything like what I had to hear and see when there. One, however, of rather a better sort I will

describe: It was at a village four miles from Matlock. The bridegroom was a working man, and I drove over with him and some friends on the morning of the wedding. Arriving at the bride's house, we set off for Church, as I supposed in my innocence. We went in a waggonette, which, to my astonishment, pulled up at a public near the Church, to put up the horse as I supposed. Not a bit of it. Into the 'pub' we all went. Each had a drink of what they chose, and, after some quarter of an hour, we all packed into our carriage again, and drove off to Church, about three-hundred yards away. I had come to take the wedding. All went well until the bridegroom put the ring on the woman's hand, when she exclaimed, 'It's not me Mister, its 'er; that's my 'usband.' 'You stupid woman,' I said, 'why didn't you say so before? pull that ring off,' which she did. 'Now, where's the right woman?' I said. Another woman came forward, as much as to say, shall I do? 'Is this the right woman?' I asked. 'Yes, sir,' said the bridegroom, and we began again, and this time all was properly done.

Back we went to the public, where we stayed some time, perhaps an hour or so. Then we went to the bride's home for dinner. Never in my life have I seen such a plum pudding, nor ever shall I again. I am certain it must have weighed six or seven stones. The first thing I did was to cut my thumb badly, which made carving very awkward. Next to me at dinner sat a 'teetotaler', who expatiated on the evils of drink. 'Look here,' he said, as he pulled a little bottle out of his pocket, 'that's the stuff to drink, taste it.' I put it to my lips; but oh, talk about

THE PARADE, MATLOCK BATH

MATLOCK BATH

spirits, it was frightful. What it was I do not know, 'spirits of something.' In front of me stood a jug full of beer, and another half full of gravy. I don't know how, but a spirit of mischief seized me; I poured half the beer into the gravy, and poured plenty over my friend's plate of beef. 'My word, master, this is good gravy' said he; 'Yes it is, have a little more,' and he did. I hope it was not wrong, but I couldn't help it, for, of all hypocrisy, I think the worst is teetotal hypocrisy.

F.J. Metcalfe (Rector of Killamarsh)

MATLOCK BATH

On the Parade there are several spa shops, or 'museums,' as they are generally designated, the windows of which are crowded with articles, natural and manufactured. These repositories form a pleasant lounge for visitors, and in the inspection of the different objects which they contain an agreeable half-hour may be spent. The Centre Museum, to which we paid a visit, is the principal establishment. In the showroom we found a choice assortment of vases, statuettes, figures, and ornaments, in spar and Derbyshire marble, with others exquisitely sculptured in Cararra and Italian alabaster. Among the chief attractions we noticed some tables executed in Ashford black marble, inlaid with wreaths of flowers worked in different coloured stones; some good specimens of minerals – native

HEIGHTS OF ABRAHAM, MATLOCK BATH

and foreign; fossils, shells, and petrifactions – or rather preparations of calcareous matter – may also be enumerated as among the objects of interest in this exhibition.

Petrifaction working, as it is called, has become an important, and certainly not the least lucrative, branch of the 'curiosity' business at Matlock, there being several wells in the tufa where this curious and interesting operation of nature is carried on. The process of incrustation is a very simple one. The articles to be operated on (embracing almost every conceivable object, but chiefly birds' nests, baskets of fruit, moss, and the leaves and branches of trees) are placed on stands, and the water that filtrates through the tufa allowed to drip gently upon them. The moisture, in percolating through the concrete mass, becomes strongly impregnated with lime, and on reaching the open air rapidly evaporates, when a calcareous deposit is formed that in time completely incrusts the object on which it falls, and gives to it the appearance and hardness of stone.

Of the constituent ingredients of those thermal springs, that have raised Matlock to the position of an inland Spa, but little can be said, no regular quantitive analysis of their chemical contents having as yet been made.

The bathing establishments are three in number; the first in point of order is, or rather was, the Old Bath, which some years ago was purchased by a joint-stock company, when a large and handsome building was commenced on the site of the old hotel, intended as a first-class hydropathic establishment, but the works have been deserted for a considerable period, the company not having had sufficient funds to carry

THE PETRIFYING WELL

CHATSWORTH HOUSE

out its plans. The hotel which preceded it was, with one exception, the oldest building in the town, and occupied the site of the first spring discovered here; the second is at the New Bath Hotel, nearly opposite the Lover's Leap; and the third in seniority, unlike the Old and New Baths, is unconnected with any hotel, being situated in the Fountain Gardens, at the north end of the Museum Parade.

There are few places in England or elsewhere that can compete with Matlock for grand and magnificent scenery – the roads are excellent, and the walks and drives in the immediate vicinity present an almost unlimited variety of aspect. Nature having done so much in this respect, the inhabitants, who are specially interested in the prosperity of the place, seem disposed to rely too exclusively upon its scenic advantages, as forming the attraction for visitors; for, with the exception of the libraries, and the re-unions at the principal hotels, the place possesses but few resources for indoor recreation and amusement. There is no promenade, concert room, or place of public assembly, consequently the visitors remain isolated in their apartments, with little social intercourse existing among them. Under these circumstances it need excite no surprise that many who, though at first charmed with the scenery, feel, after a few days' residence, a difficulty in resisting the encroaches of *ennui*. Were the inhabitants a little more public-spirited, Matlock would become one of the most agreeable places in the kingdom, not less as a permanent

residence than as a place of temporary sojourn for the invalid and pleasure-seeker.

James Croston

THE CHATSWORTH TINKER

One afternoon on my arrival at Chatsworth – the very best head-quarters that can be chosen for excursions in Derbyshire – I strolled into the beautiful Park, and found that I had it all to myself, with the exception of an old man who was plodding slowly along, pushing a little tinker's cart before him. He was rather lame, and seemed very tired; there was therefore every reason for supposing that a rest would be welcome to him. I pulled out my pocket-knife, and asked him to grind it for me. His little barrow-like machine was so arranged that the wheel in front on which he rolled it from place to place became also the wheel for turning the leather band round the grindstone. First he lifted up the lid of a box, and pulled out a piece of tin with which he scraped the mud off the wheel. Then he put on the band, began working the treadle with his foot, and very soon a little shower of sparks was flying from my knife. From time to time he left off grinding, and tried the

26

GARDENERS AND THE CASCADE, CHATSWORTH

edge on his thumb-nail. I noticed that he was thin, grey, and careworn, and that he spoke like a man of fair education and intelligence. I asked him if he travelled far.

'Not a very wide circuit,' said he, 'for I have a lame leg, and cannot go far. Besides, as you see, I am getting old. It's a bad thing to be old, sir.'

'How far do you go a-day?'

'About seven or eight miles is as much as I can do now. I go from Sheffield to Buxton – that is my round, but it takes me a long time to do it.'

'Is your home at Sheffield?' I asked.

'I have no whoam now, sir, for you see all my children are grown up and married, and they seldom come near me. So I have no whoam.'

It seemed to him quite natural that as soon as his children were able to provide homes for themselves, he should be left without one.

'But wherever I go,' continued the old man, 'it is not very easy now to get a place to sleep in. The public-houses do not want me, and I have to go to a lodging-house, where they charge me sixpence for a bed. It takes me a long time to earn sixpence, and if I did not have two or three customers on the road who gave me a little extra, I could not get along at all. When I sleep at a public-house, I am obliged to drink something, or they would not take me in, and that soon spoils the day's work.'

He now pulled out a bottle of oil from his pocket, and took a stone from his box, and began sharpening up the knife,

which he presently handed to me saying, 'There, sir, that will pare off any corn now.' The trees were all in the first fresh beauty of summer, the lilacs and laburnums were in flower, and along the road there passed a group of happy children, carrying in their hands branches of the hawthorn. They, too, in their time would desert the parent roof, and be themselves deserted, and life would seem no better a thing to them than it did to yonder poor old man, hobbling wearily along the last stage of his journey.

Through meadows bedecked with flowers, and by the side of the river Derwent, shining in the sun like the river which another tinker saw in his dream, I walked on to Darley Dale, whither I was bound on a pilgrimage to see a yew-tree, reputed to be the largest in the county, and of great age. Man's years are three-score and ten, but many such periods put together would not reckon the life of this old yew. I found it still green and vigorous, carefully guarded within an iron rail, and likely to see many changing seasons come and go long after all human beings now upon the face of the earth have passed to 'the land where all things are forgotten'. It stands a grim sentinel in the churchyard, watching the unceasing harvest gathered in, faster even than its own leaves fall. Inside the church there are records of men who died five hundred years and more ago, but the yew was a venerable tree even then.

I stood for a moment or two looking at an effigy of John de Darley, dated 1325. A little girl, the sexton's child, stepped up to me and said, 'It is John de Darley, sir. He died with his 'art in his 'and.'

THE CHATSWORTH HOTEL

'With his what, my child?' said I, all in the dark as to her meaning.

'With his 'art in's 'and,' repeated the girl. 'He was a crusader, and that was how he died.'

The figure holds in its hand some object resembling a heart, and this has given rise to the belief that the crusader took the precaution to remove that portion of his frame before laying down his arms for ever. Presently the sexton's daughter ran off to join a group which surrounded an organ-man outside. He was playing an air from *Sonnambula*, and somehow or other it had a strangely foreign sound among those fields and hills. The boys demanded the air over again, and seemed impatient of a refusal. I said a few words to the biggest of them, who was about eight years old, and he nobly took the organ-grinder under his immediate personal protection. 'They shan't hurt him,' said he; and from that moment the Italian's life was safe. Then I found a way by the side of the river to Rowsley, and so back to Chatsworth, where, at the very gates of the Park – a Park of which it is impossible ever to grow weary – there is one of the most comfortable hotels in England, close to the pretty village of Edensor. If all hotels were like this one, how little temptation there would ever be to go home! In wandering about Derbyshire the traveller will sometimes have to put up with hard fare, and may perchance even encounter unwel-

come bedfellows, such as those which Robert Curzon tells us he met with in a Coptic monastery, where the mattress was stuffed with fleas. But it is always easy to get back to the 'Chatsworth Hotel' as a centre for exploration, and there everything is so cheerful and pleasant – the dinner so excellent, the beds so clean and sleep-enticing, the entire arrangements of the house so perfect – that when, like the old tinker, I am too infirm to walk more than seven or eight miles a-day, I will go and spend my remaining years there, and recall byegone rambles under the shade of the oak-tree in front of the door, while the pretty chambermaids disport themselves in rustic dances on the lawn.

Louis J. Jennings

THE FRUSTRATED ANGLER

Wednesday, October 1st – I commenced angling operations, and never was an adventurous old angler more thoughtfully or more kindly guided and guarded than was I by my good friend, our host of 'The Isaak Walton', who is an expert fisherman, knowing most things about angling. We carried our

MONSAL DALE

luncheon with us, and fished up the Dale as far as my old acquaintance, Reynard's Cave, which has the same old look. On my last visit I was tempted to climb up to the kitchen, and thence on to the top of the hill; there was no rope to help me then as there is now, and I was young and active, having barely turned three score; but now, although I could just as easily do it – *le jeu ne vaut pas la chandelle*. We fished all day, but with no success; mine host got a brace of very small trout and I got nothing.

In the smoke-room our various daily adventures were duly discussed, and it was rather consoling to find that not one of the experts, these experienced hands, had done much better than ourselves. That smoke-room is as cosy as it is old-fashioned, with a large recess in the window, forming a comfortable seat for three or four people. Above it is a row of a dozen pewter-plates, polished as bright as silver, and in the middle is a big bright pewter-dish, kept there as a reminder of the jolly times of long ago, and not for use in these degenerate days.

> While broken teacups, wisely kept for show,
> Rang'd o'er the chimney, glisten'd in a row.

The Master laid down the law in a big armchair; the Doctor told stories from the windowseat; the Parson read interesting bits from *The Compleat Angler*; the Poet was argumentative and

THE RIVER DOVE

29

LION FACE ROCK, DOVE DALE

THORPE CLOUD AND DOVE DALE

facetious. It was soon fully understood between us that our failure to catch any fish was due entirely to the weather, and not to our want of perseverance, of pluck, of energy, or of consummate skill and knowledge. We all agreed in this, that there *are* trout and grayling both in the Dove and the Manifold, and in the united rivers, and big ones too, but they will not be caught until they choose to do so by deigning to rise at a fly, for we are all *dry fly* fishermen here.

Thursday, October 2nd – This was also a cold and windy day. The Master, the Parson, the Major, the Doctor, the Doctor's wife, and the Poet went forth to fish, full as usual of bright hope, some to the Manifold, others to the Dove. To the latter went I, and my *fidus Achates*, the landlord, went with me, he in waders, I only in my knee boots. We wanted to cross the river at a certain point, and as it was a long way up to the bridge, he made nothing of taking me on his back, and, like Friar Tuck and Robin Hood crossing the river, we must have made a pretty picture, had one of our young ladies chanced to have been there with her Kodak. He landed me safely.

There was a well-known pool where big grayling lie, but they took little notice of a fair rise of fly on the water and floating over them. An occasional rise amid-stream drew my attention. I soon had fast hold of a big fish and landed him. Of course I thought I had hold of a grayling. I fished for a

grayling, with a grayling fly, in a noted grayling hole; and yet when I landed my fish he proved to be a lovely trout, and this, be it remembered, was on October 2nd.

Mine host and I discussed the various merits of this fish – its lovely complexion, its fat and beautiful condition, its length, its breadth, its height, and its weight – and the dispute ran high on some points, I maintaining his weight to be 16 oz at least, and mine host that he was not more than 12 oz. We agreed in this, that it is a cruel law which forbids the taking of trout at such an early date.

Not long afterwards the same thing occurred again. I fished for a grayling, and again I hooked what turned out to be a beautiful trout; and so it was all the time; we could catch nothing but pesky trout, when we wanted grayling.

'The Amateur Angler'

A TOURIST AT DOVE DALE

At Tissington I stopped a little while to admire the old church, and caught a glimpse of the hall, and then proceeded without further delay to the 'Izaak Walton' inn, where the regulation-

TISSINGTON

luncheon was soon spread before me. A gay party of young ladies were seated at an adjoining table, laughing and making merry, and to look upon their fair faces was much pleasanter than eating cold beef and pickles.

For show-places, the happy hunting-grounds of tourists, I have no mind, and consequently it was not quite with the light heart which usually accompanies me on my little journeys that I marched off from the 'Izaak Walton' inn for Dove Dale. Yet it is a thing to be seen once, and not oftener, unless a person should take a particular fancy to it. Had I known before I went into it as much as I did after I came out of it, I should have sailed away in another direction, or have been guided by old Hesiod's wise proverb, which tells us that the half is worth more than the whole.

You go over the little bridge at the foot of the meadows below the inn, under the hill called Thorpe Cloud, and find the river Dove running between steep hills, which are fringed with the hawthorn and mountain ash. The path is narrow, and after passing through a swamp, ascends to comparatively dry but stony ground till it brings you opposite some rocks fantastically called the Twelve Apostles. They are more like a set of nine pins than twelve apostles. On the hill-side I found a man selling ginger-beer, who seemed to have small respect for the Twelve Apostles or Dove Dale generally, for he declared that there was not much to see, that the path became 'much worser' as you went on, and that it might be made good enough if tourists would only subscribe among themselves to keep it in order. But when one is here it is rather too late to begin the repairs. The real truth is that it is not worth

while to go much farther than the spot where the man of ginger-beer has perched himself. All the rest is mere weariness and vexation of spirit, but no one has ever had the frankness to say so, and therefore the tourist feels himself obliged, generation after generation, to go the fixed round, like a horse in a mill. Knowing no better when I was there, I pushed on, and found that the path was sometimes inches deep in mud, and sometimes under water altogether, the river washing clean over it, and leaving one no alternative but to wade – a very bad road in all respects in a wet season, whatever it may be in a dry one. In some parts of the Dale the scenery is striking, but not extraordinarily beautiful, although it has been the subject of innumerable poems and fantastic descriptions. Also, it must be confessed, there are parts of it which make very pretty pictures. But the first mile is very like all the rest, unless one can see with the eyes of the writer of a local guide-book, who says of one place: 'Descending to the river's brink, we see suspended aloft on the steep hill-side a mighty fortress, with its magnificent arched gateway, thrown as if defiantly wide open.' This fortress I could not find, perhaps because it is not there. There are some caverns on the way, easily accessible to those who care to scramble up the hill-sides in search of them. I did so in one or two instances, and sorely repented that I had taken so much trouble. At last I came to Mill Dale, a collection of tumble-down cottages and poverty-stricken people, one of the least pleasant or cheerful villages I have ever seen in England. Not far from here, at Alsop in the Dale, there once flourished a family named Alsop for many a generation. They came to this pleasant place

BONSALL

about the time of the Conquest, 'and continued,' as Lyson tells us, 'in an uninterrupted descent for nineteen or twenty generations' – a record which few existing families can equal. I now decided to strike off up the hill, by a sort of cart-track, for Alstonfield, and make my way to Hartington, from whence I proposed to make an expedition into the Dale at the other end, having had a little more than enough of it for one day.

An old church and an old hall stand looking at each other at Alstonfield, and I soon found my way into the former, which at that moment was being energetically 'restored'. The inside was a confused mass of timber, mortar, old wood-work, and rubbish. First my attention was attracted to a venerable pew, which turned out to be the identical pew erected by Charles Cotton when he was the owner of Beresford Hall. It was elaborately carved, and of good old oak, but had received a thick coat of green paint at the hands of some barbarian many years before. Then there was a very strange pulpit, bearing the date upon it of 1637, at which period the people of England were just beginning to make up their minds that their king, Charles the First, must either mend his ways or have them mended for him. The pulpit is almost as large as a room, and below it there is a reading-desk, all forming part of the same fabric, and

ASHBOURNE

LATHKILL DALE

all carved with skill and care. It was of fine old oak, and yet had actually been varnished and grained to resemble oak – one of the most curious instances I have ever seen of that depravity in the natural man which leads him to prefer the artificial to the real. Here was the genuine article, and yet it must be disguised beneath a coarse and ugly imitation of itself. Having taken a good survey of the country from the top of the church-tower, and nearly broken my neck in getting down the steep, dark, and worn belfry-stairs, I gathered myself together and started off at my best speed for Hartington, for already the shades of evening were beginning to descend upon the earth. At this critical point I fell a victim to my besetting sin, and listened to the voice of the tempter who stood as usual for me by the wayside with suggestions of short cuts and field-paths. He told me that the field-path saved at least a mile and a half, which was a consideration of some weight with me just then, for to say the truth, my stoutest boots were all soaked with the water of Dove Dale, and cut to pieces with the stones, and I wished to get as soon as possible to Hartington, whither I had prudently sent on my bag beforehand. 'You take the first stile at the end of the village, and go straight on,' said the man. I knew as well as if I had been there that it was all moonshine, and that no sooner had I committed myself well unto this field-path than it would split up into three or four, or cease altogether, or blunder into some farmyard close to a big dog, and that it would not be possible to go straight on without banging one's brains out against a barn or tumbling head over heels into some river. This, I say, I knew quite well, but the

temptation was too much for me. I am but a poor weak creature when field-paths are mentioned, and never can see one without taking to it, and thus many and many a time have I brought myself into ugly scrapes. On this particular evening, being tired and wet and hungry, it was harder than ever to resist a short cut. For some time all seemed pleasant and all went well, as it generally does when we slip out of the right way into the wrong one; but presently the daylight began to fade, and at about the same interesting moment the path disappeared also – not that it was too dark to see it, but the path itself was of a surety no longer there. Soon I found myself straggling on among browsing cattle, stone walls, and mud – tired, hungry, and out of humour. Then I struck a cart-track and kept on it, till I met with two labourers, who told me I was all right, and that I was to keep 'straight on', through a wood and across a river – all sounded well enough by daylight, but not so pleasant after dark, and in a country which one has never seen before. I went straight on, and before long was brought up plump against an old barn, where the cart-track utterly vanished, as the field-path had done before. What was to be done now? Keep 'straight on' again? What else could one do? On I went accordingly, and in a few minutes had the pleasure of finding myself deep in water and slush in the middle of a field, every step filling my boots with mud and filth. I love the country much, but to this sort of entertainment I have so strong an objection as the veriest town bird in all London. I tried back, and tried forward, but there was no way out of this slough of despond. 'Then I thought,' says John

ATLOW MILL

Bunyan, and his words were as barbed arrows to me in the middle of that field, 'that it is easier going out of the way when we are in, than going in when we are out.' Also I remembered his description of the two field-paths which enticed Christian out of the road: 'The one took the way which is called Danger, which led him into a great wood; and the other took directly up the way to Destruction, which led him into a wide field full of dark mountains, where he stumbled and fell, and rose no more.' But the recollection of these passages did not help or console me, and I continued to blunder on, tired and disgusted. When at last I got out of that field, I was heavier by a cart-load of mud than when I went into it. Then I came to a river, the Dove, and as something had been said about a bridge, I kept by the bank until I found one – a little foot-bridge, hard to discover. It was then totally dark, and there were no signs of Hartington, neither was there any light to be seen, turn whither I might. Going back was impossible, and there was nothing for it but to make a dash forward. I did so, and soon came to a check in the shape of a ditch. This I jumped, first pitching my umbrella across by way of burning my boats behind me. I alighted in the middle of some unusually well-developed stinging-nettles and some long wet grass, and then made out the outlines of another barn, towards which I bent my devious steps. I now quite made up my mind that I should have to spend the night in these delectable fields. But after dragging through another morras, I stumbled upon

the road, and all at once found myself blinking like an owl before the dim lights of the 'Charles Cotton' inn, and received a friendly greeting from the landlady, although I was covered with mud, and must have looked very like a tramp of the more dangerous description.

The landlady took me into the kitchen, where there was a good fire, around which sat a group of the villagers smoking their pipes. Then the kind hostess brought me a pair of socks, for my own bag had not been delivered by a faithless Buxton driver, and she told me they were accustomed to do this friendly turn for travellers who had been through Dove Dale, and who almost invariably landed soaking wet. 'We even lend them trousers,' said the good soul, but luckily my case was not so bad as to call for so great a sacrifice.

Louis J. Jennings

FARMERS' FARE

Food was plentiful and wholesome – no tinned food at all. When that did come in, people were afraid to eat it for quite a while, being afraid of poisoning. Oatcake, bacon and eggs, porridge made with salt and no sweetening and poured into a basin of milk were usual. There were always plenty of home-

FLAGG

made jams, and a favourite sweet was either cornflour or ground rice blancmange, turned out of a mould and flanked with spoonfuls of jam. Bread and cheese was the main supper food and also for taking out for lunch. We drank milk for supper and beer or one of the numerous home-made drinks for other liquid refreshment.

F.W. Brocklehurst

BOOTS AND SMOCKS

My father wore enormous square top hats, quite unlike anyone else's, one for the village and a best one for the market town. He was most particular about his clothes and hats, and before he went out we ran round him with brushes and whisks, my mother smoothing and brushing his hat, the servant brushing his topcoat, I whisking his trousers, and the servant boy polishing his boots.

I was the chief putter-on and puller-off of boots, and I carried them to the barn to be cleaned by the boy, and then tugged and pulled to draw them on my father's feet. I was reprimanded for my carelessness in this work, for I never unloosed enough laces, and the struggle was dour, as my father pushed and I pulled. When he returned from his journey, or from the farmwork, I sat at his feet to remove the boots. I tugged, and fell over backwards every time, rolling over the

hearthstone, as the great boot was suddenly loosened and his foot slipped out.

There was keen rivalry between my brother and myself over these boots, and we each took one foot, as my father sat back at his ease. Then we got the warmed slippers from the fireside and dragged them on. This operation always took place in the kitchen, for nobody ever went into the sitting-rooms or bedrooms in boots.

It was an important piece of work, which an autocratic man appreciated, and when we were older this duty was taken on by the servant boys.

A truly ancient man, whom everyone called 'Uncle Allsopp' although as far as I know he was no relation, used to come to see us when I was very young. He arrived unexpectedly and dramatically, riding over the hills on his pony. One of us, looking out of the windows, would suddenly exclaim: 'There's somebody riding down the Top Pasture. Is it Uncle Allsopp? It looks like his smock frock.' Then I ran outside and waited for him, and the rest of the house prepared a meal. He sat in the kitchen, with his big face wreathed in white whiskers, and I listened to his talk which I couldn't understand, for he used old words and a broad dialect. He wore a smock, snowy-white, and very beautifully worked, admired by all of us. I sat on his knee, holding his enormous stick, and smelling the harsh fragrance. Even in those days he seemed to have come out of another century. He was independent, both in means and appearance, and he refused to change his ways or bow to modern fashions. People whom he met stared at his odd figure, but he passed the

THE PARK, BELDER

time of day, and rode calmly on. He was very old, he must have been born before Trafalgar, but I was too little to ask any questions of those times. I stared at him, and fingered his smock shyly, and watched his toothless jaws. His face was ruddy and smooth, his eye like a bird's, quick, spying every-thing, his movements, though slow, had no uncertainty. He could give and take a joke, for I remember the laughter and gaiety of the venerable old man, whom nothing could disturb, until Death came and they walked serenely off together to the green fields of heaven.

Alison Uttley

EXPLOSION AT COAL ASTON

We were leaving the brilliant sunshine behind us to go down the pit. It was two o'clock and four of us were going down together. The pumps had stopped and there was water in the bottom to a depth of three feet. We had to stop five yards from the bottom and step onto a landing.

All of us were temporarily blinded with coming from glori-ous sunshine into pitch black darkness. We could not see a thing and the first man to step off met with disaster. Instead of treading on the landing he trod – on nothing, and fell into the water and the sound of splashing and curses assailed our ears.

KIRK IRETON

37

BOLSOVER

DENBY COLLIERY

He was a man who swore frequently and he roundly cursed everyone and everything in or connected with the pit.

Our eyes were becoming accustomed to the darkness and we could dimly see him spluthering about like an unwieldy frog in the water. We three who were left negotiated the landing more carefully and walked across it fifteen yards to the edge of the water. Pebow was so wet he decided to go home and his mate went as well. Now there were only two of us and the pump man left in the pit. He said he would have the water out in an hour and half. So we went to our place and we had strict orders how to work and what to do. Every twenty minutes or half an hour we had to go and fire the gas with our candles. We were working about ten yards from the coal face in a low side hole and in it had been sunk another hole to hold water. This prevented the water from getting to the coal face. It was big enough to hold a man, and it was full.

Every half hour we fired the gas but at last we became so intent on our work that the next time we remembered, we realised that it was considerably over half an hour since the gas was last fired.

I went down to light the gas and it struck off my candle a ball of fire two inches across. It was all fire.

The ball of fire went from me to the coal face where it started spinning and growing bigger until it was the size of the rising sun. It was still spinning the last time I saw it before I darted in the water hole. Except for the seat of my trousers I was completely submerged and not a second too soon for almost immediately the gas exploded. It roared past me and the part of my trousers above water was burnt away to the skin.

DENBY COLLIERY OFFICIALS

I gulped, trying to take my breath, but found I was swallowing water, so I held my breath as long as I could. It seemed to be all over in a second or two and we, being in a downhill hole, the damp went over us and up. I scrambled out and crept on my hands and knees to my mate.

He asked me, 'Are you hurt?'

'No,' I said, 'Are you?'

'No.'

He was a man about thirty years older than me and we were both in the dark. I heard him say, 'Let us creep to the wind road and keep down.'

We started. Then the manager and two other men came down the pit and running into our place they shouted, 'Are you all right?'

'Yes.'

He brought three safety gas lamps with him, the ones we should have had when we went down. He stood and looked at us and seemed astounded past belief.

'Well! I can't understand it,' he said, 'You firing that gas and not getting hurt! It smashed three doors down, two round the first turn, one round the second. Two hundred yards from where you lit it and another hundred yards on in the pit bottom, it's turned wagons upside down and what it hasn't uptipped it's blown all the coal out of them. And you've escaped!'

We learnt afterwards that the explosion had been heard half a mile away and came to the conclusion that we had not to be killed.

Joseph Sharp

[Firing gas with candles was, by this date (c. 1885), an illegal practice. In any place subject to explosive gas (firedamp) safety lamps should also have been used.]

NIGHT POACHING

Charles Keeton, John Byard, Joseph Boultbee, John Walker, Samuel Harrison, John Kinder, Joseph Bennett, and Levi Woodhouse were charged that they did, at Wingerworth, on the

WIRKSWORTH

DENBY COAL TRUCKS

21st September, 1892 (to the number of three of more together), about the hour of one in the night, being then respectively armed with certain offensive weapons, to wit, bludgeons, together did unlawfully enter a certain close of land then in the occupation of one Booth Waddington, there situate, for the purpose therein of taking and destroying rabbits. – Mr W.B. Hextall prosecuted, and Mr W.H. Stevenson defended. All eight men pleaded not guilty. Mr Hextall said the question the jury would have to decide was whether the persons were armed in the way indicated in the charge or not, and whether the men in the dock were the men concerned in the affair at Wingerworth.

At about one o'clock on the morning of the day in question the headkeeper, two underkeepers, and a watcher, were out watching upon the land in question. At about that hour they were attracted by the barking of a dog, and going in the direction of the sound they were received by a shower of stones. They had with them a number of lights called 'detective lights' being long staffs with an inflammable mechanical appliance on the top, which being ignited, flared with considerable brilliancy and disclosed all objects in their vicinity. These staffs were stuck into the ground by the watchers and ignited, and their light disclosed 14 or 15 men standing together armed with bludgeons and other offensive weapons. The lights flared for four or five minutes, and the watchers had consequently ample time in which to identify the men by whom they were opposed. That the men had been armed with stones was manifested by the fact that previous to their discovery by the watchers a shower of stones greeted the latter, and

MARKET PLACE, BELPER

they issued from the spot in which the allged poachers were subsequently found to be located. One of the keeprs was seriously hurt in the face by one of these missiles. There was a hand-to-hand fight, and the fifteen men charged the watchers two or three times, and the latter received several injuries, though, happily, no very serious ones. On the following day Kinder went to a certain man at Wingerworth and offered for sale 43 rabbits. The man to whom he offered those rabbits saw several men in the neighbourhood, evidently friends of Kinder. It would also be stated in evidence that the houses of the prisoners were visited subsequently to the occurrence which gave rise to the charges preferred against them, and it was ascertained then that every one of the eight prisoners at the bar were away from home at the time of the alleged affray. – George Murray, head keeper for Mr Wilson Mappin, who has the shooting rights at Wingerworth, stated that on the night of the date in question he was watching in the park, in company with three others, when the affray occurred as described by Mr Hextall. One of the stones struck him on the forehead, and others on the body. When the prisoners and their companions charged witness and the other watchers, they said, 'Come and let's kill the –:' The injuries to himself necessitated his confinement to bed for three days. He lived at Stocksmoor and the prisoners resided at Clay Cross. He knew them all, and they were colliers. In answer to Mr Stevenson, witness said that prisoners and the other men formed into a line, Keeton being on the left hand-side, and a little short fellow on the right. – Mr Stevenson: Who was he? Witness: He was a stranger to me, but he could aim pretty straight (Laughter).

The Court then adjourned.

Derby Mercury, 14 December 1892

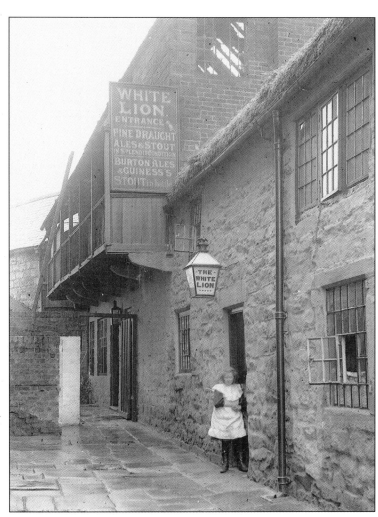

BELPER

ALBERT.WIGLEY.RSS.

SHOEING & GENERAL FORGE

BELPER

BONSALL BRIDGES

There is an old weedy water-wheel by the roadside in an artist's setting of scenery, and presently comes what was once the sign of the Pig of Lead, but is now called The Via Gellia Inn, a hostelry that reminds us that we have reached Bonsall. Shall we pursue the rivulet to the cotton-mill romance of Cromford, and the comfortable tea at The Greyhound, or desert it for the beauties of Bonsall? The difficulty of decision is a great one. Both paths have particular charms. We are in the position of the classic donkey, which perished between two bundles of equally dainty hay because it was such an ass as to be unable to determine which was the more toothsome; of De Quincey, who, having six hours to spend in London when passing through, spent them on the steps of the hotel vainly endeavouring to decide what to go and see; of the typical Englishman of the time in the old cartoon, who stands naked amid a great pile of garments, embarrassed as to what clothes he should wear. Kalmat solves the problem by a vulgar expedient – heads, Bonsall; tails, Cromford. It is heads.

A primitive little village, this Bonsall, with a hundred and fifty marble bridges. So the local joke puts it; for the rivulet, a shallow streamlet of quivering clearness, which runs down the side of the street, is crossed at the cottage doors by blocks of Derbyshire marble. Bonsall once boasted a market, and a prim market-cross climbs up from a basement of ten or a dozen steps to proudly assert the fact. But the most picturesque object in this old-world village is the venerable church, which stands upon a rocky elevation and gives its benediction over the heads of the houses that are kneeling beneath. The landscape from this tranquil churchyard on the steep shoulder of the hill, with the westering sun throwing up his last lances of light from the Wirksworth hills, and the valley lying in a shining stillness, is one of the most pleasing visions of the day.

Edward Bradbury

CHILDREN'S GAMES IN SHELDON

We did plenty of cricket; if there were six or eight of us, we would have sides, even if this meant bowling and fielding as well. We used to play football at night if it was fine and a moon at all, running till our lungs were fit to burst, sometimes with about three or four on each side. Then we would go home and drink a pint of milk before starting supper. Another night game was hare and hounds. We picked sides and tossed

BONSALL

THE SLACK CHILDREN, MIDDLETON BY WIRKSWORTH

for who should be hares and who hounds, and to help keep up on the scent the hounds would call out 'Whip, whip and holler, if you don't shout we shan't follow', and this was usually done unless the hares were hiding somewhere very near, when they would wait till the hounds had gone further away.

Marbles started about March, and finished at Easter. Anyone playing after Easter was liable to have his marbles taken as, with a shout of 'Easter dues', the other boys would pounce on them. We played by making a ring about one foot in diameter, each putting one marble in, then all going about twelve feet away to bowl up. The one bowling nearest had first go, and a good shooter could go all round the other players' marbles in turn, knocking them out, and then pick all the marbles out of the ring. On the other hand, he could shoot at the marbles in the ring and go on until he missed. A tale father used to tell in connection with marbles was of a boy who would stay late after school playing, and when he got home his mother would say, 'Where hast been till now?' and on saying, 'Playing marbles', she would say 'Hast won?' If the reply was 'Yes', she would say 'Then get thee tea and dunna be late again'. If he had lost she would say, 'Then tak thee that, and that, and that', giving him a clout with each 'that'.

Another game was Peggy. This was played with a good stout stick and a piece of wood six or seven inches long and one and a half inches thick, pointed at both ends. A ring about four feet in diameter was drawn in the middle of the road (no cars to worry about) and a line about twelve yards away from which to bowl the short stick or peggy up towards the ring. Sides were picked and one side took turns with the stick. If the peggy went into the ring, that man was out, if on the line, he had only one stroke, and if outside, he had three strokes. This was done by hitting the peggy on the pointed end and while in the air, hitting it again down the street. When he had finished, the hitter would give the other side so many strides to do it in. Then the other side would try their best to stride it, as it was a point of honour to give the other side a sporting chance. If the distance was done in the number of strides given, the man was out, but if not that number was added to the total of the side. A game something similar was Billet, a game only played on Shrove Tuesday, and then by almost all the men in the village. This was played in a field with pegs every ten yards and instead of the peggy, there was a trip or a piece of wood something like a spoon hinged to a piece knocked into the ground. A piece of wood about two inches by one and a half inches was placed in the spoon and the other end was hit. This sent the wood into the air and it was then hit as far down the line of pegs as possible and each peg was counted as one mark.

Rounders or burnt ball was a favourite for mixed sexes; a game something like American baseball on a smaller scale.

44

GAMEKEEPER'S COTTAGE, TWYFORD

This was played by picked sides, one side standing in a line with backs towards a house end, and the other side would be fielding. One pitched the ball from a distance of about six yards throwing it so that the first hitter could knock it with their hand. On hitting it they would run to first base, or, if it was caught, the side was out. One never sees these games now, which I think is rather a pity. Other games were duckstones, bows and arrows, and in winter, tobogganing all down the street . . . I have known some of the young men borrowing father's ladder, fastening it on a sledge and about six of them riding on it.

'Can ith Ring' was a common game. A ring was made about a yard in diameter in which was placed a tin can. One person was 'on' as we called it and all the rest went to hide round corners, etc. The person who was 'on' had to look till he found someone, then race back to the ring, kick the can out and be in hiding before the one found could pick the can up and place it in the ring, otherwise they would be 'on' again.

F. W. Brocklehurst

THE FARM KITCHEN

The centre of life for me as a child was the farm kitchen, where all was bustle and motion, where people passed and repassed, to save the longer journey round the house walls, on their way to farm buildings, or to water-troughs, where brilliant sunshine poured in at one open door, splashing the oak dresser and grandfather clock with light, where cool breezes fluttered at the second door, to the north, and milk-cans rattled with a gay tinkle of bells as they were lifted to the wall. From the window one saw the wide fields stretched out on the slope of the hills, a steep hillside of pasture and meadowland, with massed trees and little woods, going up to the sky. It was my world, our own farmland, and I watched the distant path to see my father and the men returning along it with cans of milk on their yokes, or going to the farm buildings with a flock of hens running after.

Inside, the room was gay with painted china, lovely patterned dishes, terracotta jugs with tiny faces on the handles, bright metals, warming-pan, horse-brasses, and polished oak furniture. There were smells of varying intensity, the scent of

THE SUNBEAM CHOIR, WIRKSWORTH

the wood-fire, and sticks in the kindling box, the sweet rank smell of rainwater, drugged with moss and ferns and decaying leaves of a past year, the strangely exciting smells of pepper and brine, of herbs and cowdrinks, of newly baked bread and strong tea, and also the animal smells which assailed my quivering nostrils, absorbing, breathing, taking in all around me — the smell of rabbits which were flung under the tallboy by my father as he hung up his gun, the smell of manure on boots, of horses and cattle, of stable and byre, all came surging into the farm kitchen, part of its life.

Every article in the cosy room had its own story, told to me many times. A deep oven built in the wall bearing a bright brass plaque with the words 'Romford Roaster, 1803', was the bread oven in my grandfather's childhood. The enormous preserving pan, half copper and half brass, large enough for a bath, was used in those days, and had been brimmed with plums and blackberries each summer ever since. No one knew the age of the brass saucepans which Patty cleaned with sand from the hillside. The heavy little fender was half a wheel from one of the first trains which had travelled on the line. The grandfather clock, with its shining brass face and round oak knobs, was almost human, for its tick changed in intensity, it spoke softly, or with insistent warning, hesitating, whispering, then hurriedly chattering to my listening ears.

The oak dresser was a most important piece of furniture, for servant men had eaten their meals at its beeswaxed surface for well over a hundred years, and the ends were scarred with their knives. The drawers were pitted with shot where a farm man jokingly aimed his gun at a servant girl at the beginning of the nineteenth century. Happily she had moved aside, and

the shot spattered the front — a warning which was pointed out to every man, to unload before he entered the house.

In the drawers were neat piles of starched linen aprons, and in one drawer my mother kept the family Bible, and the books she was reading aloud. There I once found a book called *The Mystery of a Hansom Cab*. I began to read it, at the age of six, but I had scarcely finished the first page, when my mother saw me and took it away. It was a naughty frightening book, she said, and it disappeared from the house as mysteriously as it came.

On the dresser was a row of shining white metal canisters, polished bright as silver, like everything else in our house, filled with camomile, peppercorns, and spices of many kinds. They stood in descending heights on either side of the long oaken spoon-box, and I always thought they were relations, the smallest canister being myself.

At the end of the ledge on which they stood was an enormous dark-coloured pincushion, the Mother of Pincushions, heavy as if it were filled with lead, and very old. No one moved it; it squatted like an aged fat porcupine, bristling with giant needles and pins. Even the pins were unique, for many of them had once been darning-needles. When a needle's eye was broken, my mother put a little knob of sealing-wax on the end and made a scarlet-headed pin. Many a time I watched her do this, and the new pins lived charmed lives, for they never got lost. We took the greatest care of our pins, so that they were well-known, and I could have recognized some of the older inhabitants of the pincushion in a haystack of common little pins.

Alison Uttley

CROMFORD

There was our own village, with its long street winding away up the hill, with a tap here and there for water, and the inhabitants carrying buckets to their neat stone cottages. In the market-place there was an hotel, from the door of which a fisherman with rod and creel and long waders sometimes returned my earnest gaze as I waited at the smithy. Outside the barber's little wooden house I sat half-asleep for long periods. Carts and traps, dogcarts and gigs passed by, people glanced at the little girl holding the reins, the horse nodded drowsily, and hung his head, and still I waited. At last my father came out, impatiently climbing up beside me, and before he could take the reins the pony started off for home.

My father drove to the village once or twice a week, calling to order cake for the cattle, sharps and meal, or a truck-load of coal or grains from the wharf-yard. We went at an even pace along the curving white road, a steady jog-trot, the pony never breaking into a gallop, unless we met the steam-roller, when, with a dancing sideways motion, she rose on her hind legs and threatened to kick us into the river. My father never used the whip except to draw it gently across the pony's back, as if to tickle her, 'To remind her I've not forgotten it,' said he.

He nodded and bowed to everyone we saw, the hedgecutter, the traveller, the fisherman, and I held tight to the side of the newly washed spring-cart and smiled and bowed too. With his whiplash he pointed out items of interest, the bluebells colouring the little wood, pigeons on a roof, a cat stalking a bird, for the journey was important in itself, a survey of the country. He noticed other people's crops, and their gardens, their cattle and horses, and references to this drive would be made during the following week.

'I saw so-and-so, and he looked only middling,' or 'Thomas has started to cut his corn already.'

He took saddles to be mended, and a list of household wants. He talked to men about ploughshares, and harrows and machinery, about bankrupts and sales, and he heard all the news of the outside world, emigrations and wars, of Mr Gladstone and Queen Victoria, of the Duke of Devonshire, and Lord Salisbury, of Elections and Radicals (whom I confused with radishes for a long time).

He talked of the land, of the vagaries of animals, of wind and rain and snow, recalling past deluges, and storms when

TUFA COTTAGE, VIA GELLIA

trees were blown down and cattle killed by lightning, and of sudden deaths, and deeds of violence, wondering mildly what the world was coming to. Then he chirruped to the pony, and we trundled on. It was a long morning's work, and often we didn't get back till two o'clock, so we ate currant buns as we trotted along the highway towards home.

My acquaintance with the village was chiefly what I saw from my seat in the cart or trap. I was correctly dressed in serge hat, cloak to match, and gloves, and I sat as stiff as a little ramrod, but my eyes missed nothing of the goings-on around me. The stray cats and dogs, flowers in windows, unknown children, glimpses of dark shop interiors, and steady eyes of slow-moving old men and women, I saw them all.

When I sat in the pony-trap, I held my head high, proud of my position, waiting for admiring glances at the pretty dark blue trap, with its beautiful wheels, its carriage fittings, and cushions, and silver-plated harness and lamp, but the trap was kept for drives, for visits to beauty spots, to the farms and houses of distant friends, or whenever we wished to go out in style. Saturday morning jaunts were taken in the spring-cart, massive, old-fashioned, a square coach-finished vehicle, with hand-brake by my side, and a socket for the dancing whip. I sat on the dark green seat, holding the reins, whilst my father went into druggist, or tinsmith or cooper, crying 'Whoa!' if the pony got restive and

started off by herself. Sometimes I was allowed to drive part of the way home, on the level riverside, where there was no traffic. I clicked my tongue, and clutched the leather reins, twisting them in and out of my fingers and my father's large warm hands were held over mine to guide them.

There was one shop where I always clamoured to be lifted down, so the reins were tied to the brake, and I entered the paper-shop along with my father. He went for his weekly paper and talk, for the newsagent knew more about politics than anyone. I went to see the dolls, boxes of china dolls at a penny each. There were even halfpenny ones, but these had not the serene smiles of the penny ones. I turned them over, hearing tiny wee voices cry 'buy me, buy me', hesitating, lingering, till my father told me to be quick, for we must be off, and through the crowded window I could see the pony slowly starting away by herself.

Then I rapidly made up my mind and chose one, paying my precious penny, obtained by much cajolery and promises of goodness, which 'like piecrust, were made to be broken', they said.

On the way home I would decide on the name – Hilda, or Brenda or Mabel. I thought these were high-sounding aristocratic names, not dull like our country names, Ann and Kate and Sarah.

BAKEWELL

The newspaper shop was the toyshop, the stationer's and general dealer's. All our presents for birthdays and Christmas came from Mr Green's. Velvet-framed views of our lovely hills and woods hung on the walls, and I looked at them with satisfaction. I was proud of scenes I knew so well, and glad that they should be framed in red and green plush, for I felt they were worthy.

Hoops hung from the ceiling, trays of shuttlecocks with many-coloured feathers, bundles of wooden battledores, boxes of marbles, whips and toys, and skipping-ropes were there in their appointed seasons. The shuttlecocks were exquisite things, white as new-fallen snow, or variegated like parrots or popinjays. I had no doubt of the existence of birds whose red, green and blue feathers graced the shuttlecocks I saw. I usually had a flock of these winged tops, lovely beyond words, for at the farm they were carried away by high winds, blown into the troughs, or caught in the trees. I played by myself for hours at battledore and shuttlecock, counting my highest number, unconscious that I was one of a bevy of little girls all over England playing the Easter game.

My little brother had tops and marbles, I had a skipping-rope and shuttlecock. He whipped his top up and down the paths, through the little gates, and along the stone pavements to the doors of the house, and I skipped, trying to arrive at some record, a number unheard of, unimagined. The earth wore away, stones flicked in my face, a horse walked past to watering, and each time my high number was lost. Sometimes I skipped

in the barns, dancing up and down on the stone floors without interruption, till the great bins and cheese presses seemed to be moving also. Sometimes I got the servant boy or girl to turn for me, and I hopped in the elusive lively rope.

The newspaper shop was the origin of much happiness. When I asked to go to the village with my father, a vision of the shop window floated before my eyes. It was the kernel of my desires, and when I had not even a halfpenny to spend there were many things to admire, and kind Mr Green was always ready to welcome me in and show me his latest wares — sheets of transfers to be pressed on the back of one's hand, so that a butterfly or lion was pictured there, or pages of flowery texts to be cut out and made into bookmarks and keepsakes.

Alison Uttley

No Fish in the Wye

There is a very fair inn at Bakewell, once much resorted to by anglers, but the fish are gone, and the anglers have followed them. Perhaps at the very beginning of the season a few trout of fair size may be caught in the Wye near Bakewell, but as a rule the stream is most unmercifully whipped all day long, and probably poached at night, so that the fishing is now scarcely worth wasting any time and trouble over. But there are always

BAKEWELL

rods ready for the stranger in the hall of the 'Rutland Arms,' and for the first evening of his stay he may find some amusement in trying to persuade himself that he can catch a fish or two, but he had better make all his arrangements for dinner independently of his own dish of trout. The old church is better worth a visit than the river.

Louis J. Jennings

BAKEWELL PUDDING

Some of our recipes were named after the towns or villages, and one of the most famous is Bakewell Tart. I went to school in this small market town and my father used to visit the well-known market for cattle, held on Monday mornings, when cows were driven across the narrow medieval bridge, scaring us so that we had to take refuge in the triangular niches in the bridge. There we stood, as the poor cows were hurried along by shouting drovers, and we saw the startled eyes looking at us. I was filled with sorrow for them, we always treated cows with care.

The local name was Bakewell Pudding, for the tart was really for the pudding stage of a meal and not for tea.

Cover a wide shallow dish with thin puff paste. Put in it a layer of jam, preferably raspberry, but any kind will do. It should be about half an inch thick. Take the yolks of eight eggs and the beaten whites of two. Add half a pound of melted butter and half a pound each of sugar and ground bitter almonds. Mix all well together, and pour into the pastry case over the jam. Bake for half an hour, and serve nearly cold.

This was one of our favourite dishes, but it was a rich dish for special occasions only. Eggs were plentiful and cheap, and we used them lavishly, except in winter when the price rose. In summer they were twenty to the shilling, large new-laid eggs.

Alison Uttley

[It is interesting to note the inclusion of ground almonds to the filling in Alison Uttley's recipe for this famous pudding. Cookery writer Jane Grigson believed that adding ground almonds was a Victorian modification of an older, traditional version and, she believed, a much finer one, simply flavoured with almond].

BAZAAR AT CROMFORD

On Wednesday a bazaar was opened in a large marquee on the tennis courts of the beautiful grounds surrounding Willersley Castle, Cromford, the residence of Mr F.C. Arkwright, J.P. The object is to assist in defraying the cost of the enforced extensions

DERBY

which are being made to the Cromford National Schools, the Education Department having ordered additions, play ground, &c. The cost is estimated at £750. Towards this Mr F.C. Arkwright has contributed £850. The opening day was favoured by almost tropical weather, and the attendance was fashionable and numerous. The ladies presiding at the stalls were Mrs F.C. Arkwright, Miss E. Arkwright (Wirksworth), Mrs W.H. Arkwright (the Vicarage), Mrs Dawes, Mrs Gould, Mrs Hough, Lady Lea, Mrs Nicholson, Miss Pritchardson, Mrs E. Walker (Rock House), and Mrs Young. In the evening the park and grounds were illuminated with lanterns. Mr J.H. Barnes' orchestra and the Masson Mills Band contributed the musical portion of the programme. The two days bassar held in the Willersley Castle gardens realised an aggregate of about £240.

Derby Mercury, 16 August, 1893

MISERABLE HUMP-BACKED CYCLISTS

Sir – I have written on the same subject before, and have no intention of repeating what I then said; but, if you could afford the space, I should just like to bring to the notice of those Derby cyclists to whom it applies (I am afraid they are many), the following extract from a paragraph in the *Field* of Saturday last:– 'The outrageous attitude assumed by a lot of the youths who now ride about is suffcient to bring ridicule upon any pastime, and, no doubt, it deters many from taking up cycling, owing to the entirely erroneous impression they receive that the pursuit involves the contraction of the hump-backed position of the racing man, with its permanent effect upon the deportment of those who adopt it. We do not believe in the pastime being entirely dominated, to its great injury, by racing men, who do not constitute 1 per cent of the riders. It is anything but creditable to the large numbers of intelligent men who are keenly interested in bicycling, that nothing should be done to encourage a better style of riding, and one more conducive to health, effective propulsion, and appearances, than the ungainly attitude now so prevalent.' This is only one of the many passages to the same effect which are constantly appearing in print. Unluckily they do not seem to have much effect, but the only way is to stick to it till they do. I was noticing only the other day a great number of cyclists who had ridden out into the country, and were walking about amusing themselves and I never saw such a miserable humpbacked lot of men and boys in my life. If that is the type of Englishman we are to have in the future, and it looks rather like it, then the sooner cycling goes to the dogs the better. – Yours truly,

'X'

Derby Mercury, 2 August, 1893

51

THE CAT AND FIDDLE, BUXTON

GOYT VALLEY

KINDER CLOUGH

THE CAT AND FIDDLE

The old road from Burbage does not go to Axe Edge, but brings the traveller out close upon the Cat and Fiddle, a lonely sort of inn amid a wild waste of moor, which I had hoped to make my head-quarters for a day or two. But the landlord smilingly assured me that this was impossible. Heaven had been pleased to confer upon him a large family without a corresponding number of bed-rooms, and consequently he can do little or nothing for the traveller. 'There are twelve of us here,' he told me, 'and only four bedrooms,' and after that simple arithmetical statement I did not press my request to be allowed to sleep there. It is a pity, however, that the 'Cat and Fiddle' has not even one room set aside for strangers, for every judicious traveller would desire to stay a day or two there, and examine the country round with the attention and care which it deserves. The nearest bed to the 'Cat and Fiddle,' however, is at Buxton, and that is rather more than five miles away.

The front of the house faces Cheshire, and on the turnpike road a little way below it is a stone marking the boundary of three counties – Derbyshire, Cheshire, and Staffordshire. The place is therefore rather peculiarly situated, and one would like to strike off from it as a starting point, instead of having to walk five miles to it, and then be barely at the beginning of

the real day's work. I would have contented myself for one night with the little parlour, in which there is a picture on the wall of a cat playing upon a fiddle, but the landlord begged me not to think of it. Let us hope that his house will grow large and his family remain as it is. In the meantime, the stranger may easily make an excursion to it by the way I have mentioned, or by Goyt's Clough, and having reached it, let him proceed on the Macclesfield road a few hundred yards past the inn door, when he will notice a gate opening into an old cart track. Follow this track, turning to the right, and keeping on past a shooting-box. Then go on by a wall winding up the hill to the left, and when the top of the hill is reached, a magnificent view will reward the traveller for his pains – a view extending far over Lancashire and Cheshire, and towards the Kinderscout, king of Derbyshire hills, and taking in the rocks of Beresford Dale, with many a mile of green valley and brown moorland. Everywhere the hills are broken up into scores of fantastic shapes. This is the best thing the country anywhere near Buxton has to show, and when the visitor has seen it, he cannot do better (supposing that his time is limited) than return to the Cat and Fiddle, and take the straight road to Axe Edge. It runs southward, past two or three collieries or pits, and at the brow of the hill the stranger should turn off on to the moor to the left, and make towards a pile of stones

THE CRESCENT, BUXTON

which marks the highest point of Axe Edge. The hill is long and rather steep, and here the beautiful river Dove takes its rise, as well as three other rivers – the Wye, the Dane, and the Goyt. It need scarcely be said that they make no very brave show at this height – it will puzzle the stranger even to find them all.

Louis J. Jennings

BUXTON WATERS

Buxton is not a place which the traveller or sketcher will desire to visit more than once. A French tourist who visited Buxton in 1784 (St Fond), thus records his impressions of it: 'Its waters may be excellent, but its atmosphere is impregnated with sadness and melancholy.' But the Buxton waters are justly celebrated for their healing properties, and a stranger there will come to the conclusion that they cure all the diseases known to man, for he may see them applied in an endless variety of ways. People drink them, bathe in them, and even pour them into their eyes out of little glass vessels, an operation which it makes one feel very uncomfortable to witness. Invalids crowd the streets and hotels, for the springs are said to produce miraculous effects, making the lame to walk and the blind to see. At the large hotels it is customary to dine at a fixed hour

with a collection of interesting 'cases,' all of which the visitor will sincerely hope will have a favourable termination, while heartily wishing himself away from the scene. Once I tried a smaller inn in order to escape the necessity of studying chronic forms of rheumatism and gout, but I was rather taken aback by a man informing me confidentially as I sat smoking my cigar in the parlour that when he was last there he had been tormented by 'boogs'. 'They bite me i' th' eye, and boong 'em a' up,' said he, and I was nearly decamping on the spot, but there turned out to be no occasion for alarm. It does not need a visitation of this kind to depress one's spirits in Buxton, for in bad weather everything is calculated to produce that effect – the long processions of invalid-chairs, the eye-washings, and the clouds which too often gather from all the neighbouring hills, and pour out their contents upon the town. I have been there on several occasions, and never saw the sun shining three hours together, but doubtless old inhabitants can remember days when it has been visible all the morning, or perhaps during an entire day, although it would require a considerable body of evidence to induce me to believe it. At night how the windows rattle all over the house, and by day how the keen bitter winds must rack the bones of all who are condemned to inaction, or to be dragged up and down the cheerless streets in Bath-chairs! The authorities of the town have done all that is in their power to render it attractive – it is exceedingly well kept, there is a good concert hall, a garden which must be a pleasant place to lounge in when the weather is favourable,

GLOSSOP LAMPLIGHTERS

good shops, and clean streets. The hack drivers are numerous, and seldom ask more than twice their proper fare. But when all is said, the man who is not in need of medicinal waters will shift his quarters as soon as he has explored the country round about, and this will provide him with occupation for a day or two, most of the excursions taking him a safe and comfortable distance beyond the town.

Louis J. Jennings

TREATMENTS AT BUXTON SPA

Acute gout is benefited by drinking the thermal water, but bathing should not be permitted. The local vapour bath is, however, most efficacious, the affected joint being placed in the box at a temperature of from 115° to 120° for ten to fifteen minutes, once or twice daily. As the inflammation subsides, and the disease becomes subacute, a mild, mineral bath at a temperature of 95°–97° may be taken after the application of the vapour, which should then only be given on two days out of three; the douche should not be used at first, as its pressure is apt to cause recurrence of the local inflammatory trouble.

In irregular, suppressed, or latent gout, or in the condition known as 'goutiness,' it is best to begin the course with the

ST ANN'S WELL, BUXTON

ILKESTON

'combined baths,' the vapour portion of which may be given 'full' or 'half' as thought best. After these have been taken for a period of from four to fourteen days, the immersion bath may be taken at a lower temperature, or better still, the 'natural' bath, if its use is not contra-indicated; return being made to the combined bath if pain comes on. The water should be drunk twice or three times daily, preferably with the addition of the morning saline.

In chronic cases, with hepatic torpidity, lymphatic engorgement, and thickening of joints, the massage bath is of great value.

In the acute form of rheumatism no baths can be taken, but the waters should be drunk, and great benefit is often obtained from a wet blanket pack. In chronic rheumatism, warm immersion baths with under water or direct douching, massage baths, and natural bath are most effective.

In sciatic neuralgia, half combined baths with the hot under-water douche, massage baths, and sinusoidal electric baths are indicated, with or without stretching of the affected nerve: and during the latter part of the course, the natural swimming bath.

Dyspepsia and Hepatic Torpidity: drinking of the thermal waters with a saline in the early morning. Massage baths with the Aix douche, and the application of packs of mustard bran over the liver and stomach, are indicated here.

Obesity: the waters as above, massage baths, combined baths, and high frequency currents.

Affections of skin: drinking of the waters, combined baths, and in some cases sinusoidal baths, or high frequency currents.

Spinal and Nervous Affections generally. The tonic mineral baths, the various forms of electrical massage, and hydropathic treatment, needle baths and Scottish douche; in cases where a 'specific' factor is present, the Aachen treatment by warm sulphur baths, and mercurial inunction should be given.

Cardiac Affections: if gouty or rheumatic, the drinking of the thermal water; sometimes a very mild massage, or three-quarter immersion bath, or the local application of vapour to an affected limb or joint, are distinctly helpful.

Malaria: drinking of the thermal water, the massage bath, packs of mustard bran over spine and liver, plain or electrical massage.

William Armstrong and J.E. Harburn

HARVEST TIME

Uncle John's family and ours used to join together for haymaking. Our land for haymaking was close to Uncle John's

QUARNDON

land, and it was not much trouble to go from one field to another. Our father did the mowing and hacked the wall sides, pitching the hay on, stacking, etc, while we children raked the backswath for the mower, tedded round the walls, and did most of the swath-turning and loading, stopping now and then at corners to count the blisters. Uncle John's fields were very small, sixteen acres in thirteen fields, so there was quite a lot of wall sides and corners for so small an acreage.

All the farm children worked hard in the hay, and usually enjoyed it, having rides in the carts and having good feeds in the open, although we often got blisters on our feet carrying the food and drink from home. The carts had shelvings, but no gormers (end pieces) to hold the hay on, and we learned at a very early age how to build a load that would carry. We used to put one forkful at each corner in front and a good one to hold them on, the same was done at the rear, then two more were placed on one side to bind the side on and one in the middle. The same was done the other side and we then filled all the centre of the load. This was repeated about four times and one had to judge where the load was by looking where the horse's head was. All loading was done by hand, no forks, the hay being rolled into a sort of ball and built like bricks. This made it easier to unload, because if the hay was long it could save a lot of pulling and tugging if the thrower off knew just which place to form off next.

We always had a few acres of oats, all cut by scythe until I left school. When they were ripe and ready to cut, father would cut a swath across a piece (depending on which way the straw fell straight). It was then taken up by hand and if the straw was long enough, he would pull a few straws out of the end of the sheaf to tie with, otherwise a band was made by twisting the heads of a few straws together and laying it on the ground to put the sheaf on. It was my first job, after raking clean with a hand rake, to make bands till father finished mowing. Then he would take the corn up and put in on the bands while I tied the sheaves. When stooking we always put five sheaves each side for a kiver with two sheaves upside down on top to protect the oats and tied together to hold them firm. Two of these kivers of twenty-four sheaves we called a thrave, and the usual price for contract work was 3*d* a thrave. It was better for contract work if there was a bit of weed, twitch or clover in the bottom, then two cuts of the scythe made two pick-ups from the swath and a sheaf. A fast worker could do a thrave in a quarter of an hour, which was 1*s* an hour and good money when wages were 18*s* per week.

Later on we cut with a mowing machine with reaping attachment, leaving the corn in small heaps ready to be tied up, and we got help, if possible, to tie up. A man and two horse teams came from another uncle's farm, the man driving and putting the corn off at the same time. He used a short wide rake which he kept bringing forward to pull the corn back on to a rack at the back of the cutter bar. When the foot was pushed down, the back of the rack was raised, so that it caught the corn, then every two or three yards the foot was

SHELDON

raised and the rake held on to the corn heads, so that the corn slipped off ready to be tied up. I did the same afterwards with a one horse machine and the only thing I had to watch was when the horse made a grab for the corn, and pulled the machine too near. After finishing cutting, one or two would go milking, while the others would stay stacking and finish what was cut. We always counted how many thraves we had done, so that when a man who helped us went to the Devonshire Arms for a drink afterwards, he could do a bit of bragging about it. He would give a preliminary cough and then say 'We cut so and so today'. 'You never did!' was echoed all round and cries of unbelief, especially from old William, the man who worked on the farm at the Devonshire Arms. There is quite a lot of jealousy about finishing first on farms, although at the time, those who did finish first usually went to help those who had not.

If father was corn cutting while I was at school, I would ask to go at a quarter to four, just before prayers, then run on to the moor to help stook the day's work, usually about twenty thraves and then walk back to tea.

Not many potatoes were grown, just a few rows for the house and a few bags for neighbours. I remember as a small boy, picking the potatoes up as father dug them out. There was a keen frost and a thick fog, so I was very pleased when father said we would go home as my hands and feet were about frozen.

No artificial manures were used, but a lot of fields were limed and sometimes slag or ground bones were used. We did not like the ground bones as they were not steamed or sterilised, and it was thought they brought disease. On Sheldon Moor there are lots of disused small lime kilns, about four on our land. The idea seems to have been that it was cheaper to cart coal from the pits sixteen miles away, dig stone anywhere, make a lime kiln, then put first a layer of coal and then of stone, till the kiln was filled. It was then lit underneath, a passage having been built to the bottom of the kiln. Then it was left till it burnt out. The lime was taken out at the bottom, some kilns holding four or five tons, others ten or twelve. The inside of a kiln is from three to seven yards wide at the top tapering down to a point where a hole is left to get the lime out. I suppose the old farmers had realised that the liming caused the oats to ripen earlier and were of better quality. I remember most of the farmers sending oats to the mill to be made into oatmeal for home use. When the oatmeal came back it was tasted and commented on by any farmers who called, and we children used to eat the dry meal with sugar, so it was a great thing if nice flavoured.

F.W. Brocklehurst

STONEY MIDDLETON

PLAGUE VILLAGE

Derbyshire villages are not often very picturesque, and many of them will recall to the stranger the miserable places which abound in the West of Ireland. Stoney Middleton is not attractive; but it stands almost at the gate of a very fine valley, guarded by a precipitous rock, from the top of which, as the story goes, a love-stricken young woman once threw herself in despair. This no doubt was an effectual remedy for love, but so is time, as the young woman would have found if she had only waited patiently. From this point onwards the rocks are massive and grand, standing high above the road, and broken into shapes suggestive of old castles, or dilapidated mansions, or a ruined church. One of them is known as Castle Rock, another as Church Tor, and a stranger who saw them for the first time would find it easy to believe that they were the remains of buildings made by man rather than natural formations of limestone. There are caverns beneath the rocks, and in some places a little gallery, half-way up, along which the curious sightseer may cautiously creep. Close by an inn near the centre of the vale there is a road leading to Eyam, another somewhat melancholy village, but not on any account to be passed by unvisited, for there is much beautiful scenery round about it, and the place itself is associated with a touching and memorable story of suffering and devotion. The streets have now a grass-grown appearance, many of the houses and cottages are left empty or in ruins, and the only pleasant-looking spot in it

is that upon which stands Eyam Hall – a comfortable old English home, with a garden laid out in antiquated lawns and terraces. One almost expects to see a gay party of cavaliers and maidens step out from behind a hedge, and gather the flowers which bloom as they did in the self-same garden more than two centuries ago.

While looking at the outside of the church, and admiring the fine old cross in the churchyard, a boy offered to go and find the sexton. But it turned out that the sexton was at that moment deep in a grave, from which secure retreat it was difficult to dislodge him, and therefore the boy brought his wife in his stead. She was a plain and simple woman, bearing upon her face the marks of a hard life, and, perhaps, more than her fair share of trouble. She told me that one of her sons was at home, but had only earned 2s 3d in two weeks. He was a shoemaker by trade, the making of shoes being one of the staple industries of Eyam, and lead-mining the other. But for some time past both have been in a bad way, for nobody seems to care to buy the shoes, and the lead is no longer in demand. 'Lead is so cheap,' said the woman, 'that they cannot earn anything by working at it. Our trade is all gone.'

Thus saying, she opened the door of the church, the most interesting feature of which is an aisle to the memory of the Revd W. Mompesson, who laboured among the plague-stricken community here throughout the year of terror, 1665, when, out of the 350 inhabitants of Eyam, 267 perished miserably, and were put to rest beneath the fields which they had

59

EYAM

tilled. In one field there is a stone over a family of seven persons, all of whom died in a week, and were dragged, as tradition says, to this spot by their mother, and there buried. The stones over their remains are still to be seen. Mr Mompesson closed his church and held service in the open air, in a lovely ravine, and isolated his unhappy parishioners so that the contagion should not spread. It was his mournful lot to see his own wife fall a victim to the scourge, but he never ceased to do his duty, endeavouring to the last to turn the thoughts and hopes of his poor people to the only sure and unfailing source of comfort under all sorrows and disasters. The aisle, which is dedicated to this faithful follower of his Master, is scarcely worthy of his name, and the ancient cross outside might have been made a more suitable memorial to both husband and wife. There is a stone over Mrs Mompesson's grave, with her name inscribed upon it. 'I have cleaned the letters out with a stone very often,' said the sexton's wife, 'but the moss soon fills them up again. As I was telling you, sir, I have a son in India in the 17th Hussars, and last May another one, a third, enlisted in the artillery. It is very hard.'

'But not harder,' said I, 'than to make shoes at Eyam which nobody will buy.'

'No, sir, but it is hard to bring up sons and then lose them.'

As we came out of the church a gentleman spoke to me, and kindly offered to lend me the key of the gate which leads into 'Cucklet Delph,' the ravine in which the good parson

held his services when the virulence of the plague no longer permitted the people to assemble under a roof. This gentleman proved to be the owner of the old house above, Eyam Hall, and he very kindly allowed me to see that, and also gave me the key to Cucklet Delph, towards which I made my way through the long wet grass and over pools of water. Close by the gate of the Delph may be seen another relic of the old village – the parish stocks. The ravine below is full of wild flowers and singing birds, and the rock from which Mr Mompesson preached is still to be seen, the open space near it being known to the villagers as Cucklet Church. It is a scene now which may interest a passing artist, but these peaceful hills have witnessed the utmost extremity of human anguish and horror, echoing night after night, and day after day, with the sobs of the broken-hearted, and the cries of mothers weeping for their children, torn so cruelly from their arms.

Louis J. Jennings

EDENSOR AND THE CHATSWORTH HOTEL

Edensor at once bespeaks itself a model village, a kind of sanitary Eden, where everything is new, and stiff, and stately, nothing antiquated, free, or naturally beautiful, or that looks as

PLAGUE SERVICE IN CUCKLET DELPH

if it ever would become so. The houses are all arranged with mathematical order and regularity, and even the little patches of garden seem as if they had been laid out with the aid of a rule and compass. The inhabitants are chiefly persons employed upon the Chatsworth estate, and their dwellings, which were erected at the cost of the late duke, are all built in the ornamental villa fashion, the Anglo-Italian, Swiss, and Gothic being the prevailing styles. Each house has a small garden attached, planted with shrubs and evergreens, and adorned with roses, hollyhocks, and other flowers. The place has certainly a pretty appearance, but it lacks that charm and interest which some of our less pretending, but more homely and antiquated country villages possess. We love to see the old-fashioned black-and-white timber-houses, recalling the days of our forefathers, with their high-peaked gables and quaintly-ornamented bargeboards, their thatched roofs and clustering chimneys peeping out from amid their screen of leaves, their walls draped with ivy, and overhung with roses and honeysuckles and sweetbriars, looking so cosy and snug and comfortable, and speaking so unmistakably of the happiness and contentment that reigns within.

The Chatsworth Inn, near the Swiss Lodge, is a large establishment, where superior accommodation can be obtained, and being contiguous to the park gates it is very convenient for parties visiting the hall. The church and the parsonage are the only buildings that boast of any considerable antiquity. The former is a venerable structure, standing at the further end of the village, and occupies an elevated plot of ground environed by a belt of wide-spreading trees. The old church was taken

EDENSOR

THE GREAT CONSERVATORY, CHATSWORTH

CHATSWORTH

down a few years ago, and the present structure, which was completed in 1870 from the designs of Sir Gilbert Scott, was erected on its site. It is an elegant Gothic building, comprising a nave, with side aisles, chancel, and monumental chapel, with a lofty tower and spire flanking the western end. The interior contains several memorials of the Cavendish family.

James Croston

JOSEPH PAXTON OF CHATSWORTH

The sixth Duke was the patron of Paxton – Sir Joseph Paxton, MP, as he afterwards became – whose memorial tablet in Edensor Church makes the large claim for him that 'through the influence of his work and writing he has added to the charm of gardens in all countries.' Paxton was born of poor parents in 1803 at Milton Bryant, in Bedfordshire. As a boy he ran away from an uncongenial apprenticeship and was found on the road by a Quaker named Hooker, who kept the nursery gardens at Chiswick. One of Hooker's patrons was the Duke of Devonshire, who took a fancy to the young gardener and told him casually that, if he wished it, he might have a place at Chatsworth. A few hours later Paxton set off from London in

THE VICTORIA REGIA HOUSE, CHATSWORTH

the Yorkshire coach, and arrived at Chesterfield at three in the morning. He walked the nine miles from Chesterfield to Chatsworth, climbed over the wall, reconnoitred the grounds before anyone was stirring, and then presented himself at the housekeeper's room for breakfast. And before the meal was over – so legend saith – he had made up his mind to accept the Duke's offer, to remodel the gardens, and to marry the house-keeper's niece. And so he did. Joseph Paxton was a very clever man, clever himself and clever in making use of other people's cleverness, which is, perhaps, the greatest proof of brains a man can give. He has monopolised all the glory of designing the Crystal Palace – in the Chatsworth district there is a clearly marked feeling that others possessed at least as good a title as he to a share in the *kudos* of its construction. Report speaks of a certain John Marples, who was one of the Duke's agents, an uncultivated genius, after James Brindley's fashion, who knew nothing of science and rules, but could conquer any engineer-ing difficulty by sheer native ability and the application of com-mon sense and experience.

The Great Conservatory at Chatsworth is usually spoken of as the building which suggested the Crystal Palace. That is an error. The real prototype is the small Lily House, which stands before the head-gardener's villa, by the kitchen garden in the park. Paxton was one day talking with Marples and, pointing to this Lily House, said, 'Could you build it from here to

Chatsworth?' 'Certainly,' answered Marples. 'Then it's done,' said Paxton, and slapped his leg. And so the idea of the Crystal Palace was born. Paxton had the inspiration, but Marples translated it into glass and iron; and when difficulties in the actual construction arose Marples solved them. Nor is it any detraction from Paxton's fame that he should share it with another.

Paxton laid out the Italian gardens fronting the river, and his name is indelibly associated with the whole hundred and twenty-six acres of pleasure grounds, with the Victoria Regia House, and the Great Conservatory. There is, to my mind, a touch of megalomania in this colossal glasshouse, and it only bores me to be told of its miles of piping and its acreage – or is it mileage? – of glass. The sixth duke used to drive a little car-riage with four ponies and outriders through this conservatory, and he had milestones – think of it! – in his garden walks to tell him how far he was from home. This from the Whig noble, whose bust graces a real antique pillar from Sunium! Well, we all have our foibles, and, after all, the sixth duke was devoted to books and art, and, like all the Cavendishes, was a great nobleman and great gentleman. He made large additions to the library, which dates back in part to the time of Hobbes, and is specially rich in MSS and in Shakespearian quartos and folios. As for the house itself, which is most generously shown to the curious and thronging public, I have no room to

BEN STONE, CHATSWORTH GAMEKEEPER

THE DUKE OF DEVONSHIRE'S SHOOTING PARTY

describe its contents, and are they not described in all the books, both great and small? Moreover, I always find that going over these lordly houses – as one of 'a party' – is a most chastening experience. You wish to linger, but must not; the guide shepherds you from room to room, and the tired finger indicates, and the uninterested voice describes, the things in which you take not the least concern. A canoe given by the Sultan! A malachite clock presented by the Emperor Nicholas! A magnificent set of ivory chessmen! *Ohe! Jam satis est!* These things move me not. I always think of the hours I might spend there with the right *cicerone* – at leisure and in quiet.

J.B. Firth

DEATH OF A GAMEKEEPER

The village of Beeley, and indeed the whole of the Chatsworth estate has suffered a great loss in the death of Mr Benjamin Stone. He passed peacefully away on Sunday, at the age of 73, after a short illness of twelve days during which he suffered very great pain. The deceased leaves a sorrowing widow, four sons, and one daughter, with whom the greatest sympathy is expressed.

The deceased was born on the estate, and he never worked for any master other than a Duke of Devonshire. During his lifetime he served under four Dukes. No servant could have served his masters more loyally and faithfully than did Benjamin Stone. That loyalty and faithfulness was always thoroughly appreciated at Chatsworth, where the deceased was a great favourite. In youthful days he was employed in various capacities on the estate. About forty-four years ago the deceased was made a gamekeeper and in this position he lived chiefly at Beeley Hill Top.

He was a terror to poachers, with whom he had in the course of his duties many a conflict. The most serious struggle took place about twenty years ago, the facts of which will be remembered by readers of *The Derbyshire Times*. Benjamin Stone, with two or three other assistants, encountered a large Chesterfield gang during the night near the Ring Pond in Chatsworth Park. They were completely outnumbered and brutally assaulted. Stone was left on the ground for dead, and, indeed, for many days afterwards his life was despaired of. He managed, however, to crawl to Chatsworth and give the alarm. By telegram news was sent to the Chesterfield police, and by the time the poachers were approaching the town the police were alerted and captured most of the members of the gang.

During the last few years Stone retired from the post of gamekeeper, and had been engaged at Chatsworth in showing

WHITFIELD FIFE AND DRUM BAND

visitors round the House. The deceased was a native of Beeley, being the son of the late Mr and Mrs John Stone, the former being in business as a mason and builder. The deceased's wife was a Miss Prince, of Stanton-in-Peak and of the marriage there were five sons and two daughters, four of the former and one of the latter being still alive.

His mortal remains were laid to rest in the peaceful churchyard at Beeley, amid many tokens of respect, on Wednesday. The funeral was one of the largest ever seen at Beeley. As the sad cortege wended its way to the Church, where the first part of the service was held, blinds were drawn all along the route as a mark of the respect and affection in which the deceased was held. The impressive burial service was conducted by the Vicar, the Revd J. Hewitson.

The Derbyshire Times, 4 November 1911

VILLAGE SCHOOL

The question of my schooling troubled my parents, for the distance from both villages was long for a small child. Also, if I went to our own village I should have to walk by the side of the treacherous river, and maybe I should fall in and be drowned. There was a school in another valley, separated from us by a long hill whose sides were clothed in dense woods. It was finally decided to send me there, for although the way was lonely, and I should see nobody at all until I reached a tiny hamlet, I should get a better education.

The schoolmaster was famous in our district for his strictness and discipline, and for his learning. He had letters after his name which impressed everyone; he was a lecturer and musician. My mother went to see him, and explained the difficulties of the journey. It was arranged that when I got wet through I should be dried by his fire, and that in the middle of the morning I should go to his house for hot cocoa. I must take my dinner with me and eat in the schoolroom by myself. I might go for my music lesson in the next village during school hours, and on winter's nights I could take a lantern and leave school before the other children. The headmaster insisted that I should never be late, he attached great importance to punctuality, and he caned all late-comers. I must not stay away for bad weather, only illness was excusable.

I was very much excited at the prospect of school, where I should meet other girls and boys, and perhaps learn Latin and French – for our ideas of village schools were vague.

One day in spring, with a little blue linen bag containing my dinner and a pencil 'poppet', the latter of great age, I started off through the woods and the fields, and along the unknown white road to the distant school, where the bell tolled like a church bell, summoning the children from three small villages. The school was a long, low, ivy-covered building, on a hillside far from any houses, but midway between the three hamlets. Here and there in the fields and on the opposite hillside were cottages, and far away behind the curving hills

SHIPLEY SCHOOL

were other dwellings from which children came, farmhouses, watermill, inn, a scattered population of country folk.

It was a strange country to me, for although I had driven with my parents along the winding road to visit our friends at a beautiful old Hall, one of the loveliest farms I knew, I had never known anything of the cottages and their inhabitants. I felt cut off from my home, hidden from sight behind the great hill, which stretched away in the distances with its trees and rocky fields, an uncharted wood which had no paths except the one I used. My mother and I walked along the road, which curved round the base of this hill, and as we went she talked of the school and my behaviour there. I must wear a hat when I played, I mustn't sit on the cold stones, I must come straight home, and she would send the servant to meet me in the wood for the first few days.

I was impressed and pleased as I went through the big gate with its round stone balls, and its flight of broad steps which led to the playground. The school had a certain importance, with its long church-windows and heavy door. It was sheltered by a shrubbery of laurel, acacia and beech, and flower beds full of many-coloured blossoms, roses and pansies and sweet-peas, stretched under the dark walls. Next to the school lived the schoolmaster in a pretty gabled house. These two buildings, together with the infant school, the chapel and the minister's

house were a community in themselves, alone on the hillside with a heatherclad hill behind them and fields spreading out at their feet. I was delighted at the prospect around me, and I hung up my cloak and hat and dinner bag, kissed my mother good-bye, and followed a mistress into the room.

All my senses were assailed at once, and I was a wild animal caught in a trap as I realized I was alone, cut off from my mother, left in a noisy horde of children who all stared at me and whispered. I looked back at them with frightened eyes, inhaling the odour of the strange place, the coke stove, the chalk, the teacher and children, sweet-sour, harsh, and acrid smells surrounding me. There was a picture hanging on a black-board of a peacock, and a pretty girl talked to the youngest children about this bird. I stared at this row of tiny creatures, even smaller than myself, among whom was the schoolmaster's baby boy, with long golden ringlets and a lace collar over his velvet dress. I was reassured by this vision of loveliness, but when I was told to sit down by the child I felt humbled. Surely I wasn't to be among the babies, I, who could read and write and do sums?

The stern looking little schoolmistress beckoned me to her desk, and every head turned to watch me go.

'How old are you?' she asked, gazing at me over her spectacles.

DERBYSHIRE ENTOMOLOGIAL SOCIETY

'Seven,' I answered in a whisper.

'Seven years old, mam,' she corrected me, writing down my answer in a book.

'When were you born?' she continued.

'On a Saturday, mam,' I replied. It was my sad fate. 'Saturday's Child has far to go,' and I hoped no one would find out about it. However the mistress had asked me, and doubtless she wished to know whether I was 'Full of Grace or Fair of Face'.

She gave a little laugh and did not write down my reply. 'When is your birthday, child?' she asked.

'A week before Christmas, mam,' said I. She closed the book and sent me to my place, and I realized I had not made the correct replies.

The pretty teacher sat by me and asked if I knew the alphabet, and when I reassured her, very shyly, she brought a reading book and asked me to read about ab and ad. I read these queer words glibly, and she turned over, giving me longer words. When she saw I could read easily she had a whispered consultation with the mistress and I was moved to a higher class.

It was a writing lesson, and I saw slates and pencils around me. I opened my pencil poppet and drew out my quill pen. I had secreted it from the parlour, where a pile of quills lay ready on a bureau. My mother often used them when she wrote, and I thought I would impress my new school by using one too. The mistress gave a little cry when she saw it in my hands. She took it away and went to the desk. The two teachers whispered together and looked at me. It was an unfortunate beginning, and I hung my head with shame. I had done something wrong again, and I didn't know how to behave. No pens were used by little children; I must bring a slate pencil next time, said the teacher. She gave me a slate, smelling queerly of humanity, but with a good smell, too, like a windy hill, and a cold touch under my fingers. Somebody lent me a stub of pencil, but I saw in children's hands the prettiest slate pencils with red, purple, and green flowered papers round the stems. I glanced aside at these, and met the curious stares of little girls and boys, boys with white turned-down collars, girls in clean pinafores.

Then came another difficulty. To clean a slate one should have a bit of damp sponge, and I had nothing. I watched the others unctuously wash their slates and polish them, but no one offered to lend me a rag. A child spat upon his slate, and rubbed it with his cuff. I stooped over my slate and shut my eyes. Then I licked a portion with a curling disdainful tongue. Wild horses would not make me spit. I lifted up my frock and

68

THE CLOCK HOUSE AND CANAL WHARF, LITTLE EATON

rubbed the slate with the hem. I was saved for that day, and to-morrow I would bring a much nicer sponge then anyone else, I comforted myself.

We did sums, far easier than those I had done with my mother, and as I rattled off the answers, the children on both sides leaned over and copied off my slate, to my satisfaction.

Then we had reading, and I received a blue-backed little book, passed along the line, for we stood in a row for our reading lesson. It was the story of plum stones. I read the story to myself and turned over, but was promptly told to turn back. Each child struggled with the words, stumbling over the story of a little girl who went upstairs with a plate of plums. On the way she ate one, but the tell-tale stone gave her theft away. For days we lingered over this story, so that it was torture to me to hold a book containing a galaxy of tales, and never to be allowed to read any others but the silly tale of plum stones, and I sighed inwardly as the little girl walked up interminable stairs carrying her plate.

Alison Uttley

TRAMPS

Some experiences of my dealings with tramps and beggars may serve to help, warn, and interest my readers. Here are some sample cases: –

1. One day a man called at my lodgings and said, 'Your name, sir, is Metcalfe, Revd Metcalfe I should say,' 'Yes,' I said. 'You have a brother, sir, at Leeds, a choir man at S. John's Church,' 'Yes,' I replied again. 'Well, sir, he is a very kind friend of mine, and has paid my fare from Leeds to here and for my wife and three children. He told me to call on you and say that if you will pay us to Derby, he will repay you.' Having my brother's name so pat, of course I believed him, and did as he asked. When he left me he went to Derby, called on a vicar there, and said he was a friend of mine, asking him to frank him and family to Birmingham. This the vicar did; at the same time he wrote to me saying, 'I have sent your friends on to Birmingham, I hope it is all right.' I wrote back, 'Well, I am pleased someone has been taken in as well as myself.' This clever beggar performed this trick successfully till he reached Southampton, or one of the southern seaports, where he at last got caught and sent to jail.

2. 'Good morning, sir,' said a man to me, on the road one day, 'I hope you are well, sir, I don't expect you remember me.' I said, 'I had not that pleasure.' 'No, sir; no. I didn't expect you would remember me, but eighteen months ago, sir, you were kind enough to give me eighteenpence.' 'Oh indeed,' I said, 'I suppose you want another?' 'Well, hi, no, sir! not exactly, sir, I only wanted to thank you for your kindness, which I didn't do then, as I saw the Bobbie coming, and I knew he wanted me. Ah, sir,' he continued, changing his tone, 'I've been in gaol ever since then, for he caught me at the sta-

COAL WHARF, LITTLE EATON

BAKEWELL MILL

MASSON MILL WATER-WHEEL, CROMFORD

tion, and when I came out yesterday, I ses (pulling an awful face) to my poor wife, who was at the gate to meet me, Mary Ann, what we're to do now?' 'Eh, Bill,' ses she, 'hadn't yer better go and see that kind gentleman as gave yer that eight-eenpence?' 'Eh, my lass, so I will.' 'No, sir,' he said, resuming his nonchalant air, 'I want to start and get an honest living, I do indeed, only I want a start.' 'Come in and tell me what you propose to do,' I said, arriving at my lodgings. 'Where's Mary Ann?' 'She's here,' he said, and Mary Ann came forward from behind a hedge; Mary Ann was quite a clean, tidy woman. We all went into my room, where my landlady was preparing my dinner. 'Would you kindly ask the Lady to leave the room,' said the man, and my Lady bounced out in a rage. 'Now, sir,' he said, undoing his waistcoat, and pulling up his shirt, and showing me his flesh just above his left hip, 'here are two let-ters tatooed on me;' and so there were, two capital letters B C. 'That means,' he said, 'Bad Character,' and was put on when the Bobbie caught me, because I had deserted from the army. The Bobbies know that's there, and one of them said last night to me in Chesterfield, 'you've got B C on your skin.' I flew at him, knocked him down, and knocked two teeth down his throat, and got away.' 'Well, what do you intend to do?' I asked, 'Well, sir, me and my wife is going to Alfreton, and we are going to make skewers and tins and brushes, and if you'll

just lend us enough to make a start, I'll make you the most beautiful clothes brush you ever had, with a looking glass in the back; and every Sunday night my Missus shall come to your church, and bring you half what we earn in the week, till you're paid, if you'll just give us a start.' 'How much do you want?' I said. 'Well, about 11s 6d will do.' 'Now listen to me,' I said, 'Either you are telling the truth, or a lie, and if I help you, it is because I want you to have a chance to gain an hon-est living;' so I gave him the money. He had not gone many yards away from the gate, when I saw a Bobbie suddenly spring on him, handcuff him, and lead him off again, Mary Ann following in a sobbing condition. What became of the money I never heard.

F.J. Metcalfe (Rector of Killamarsh)

A MATLOCK LADY AND HER SERVANT

At the Wirksworth County Court, on Thursday, Minnie Froggatt, Gladstone Place, Matlock Bank, sued Mr John Frederick Terry, Matlock, solicitor, for £1 13s 4d wages due, and there was a counter claim for £1 through breakages. Mr

MATLOCK BATH

THE FERRY, MATLOCK BATH

M.E. De Severne, Wirksworth, appeared for the plaintiff, and Mr Terry conducted the defence. Plaintiff said she was engaged by Mrs Terry as domestic servant on November 25th last, and remained there until December 22nd. On that day she was accused of theft and dismissed. He wages were £10 per year. They declined to give her anything when she left. The counter claim was for £1 damage done to a plate-glass window, which plaintiff broke, as she alleged, accidentally. In the course of examination it transpired that she was cleaning the window, and was using a jug to throw on the water. The jug handle came off, and the vessel broke the window. It was contended the girl went a month on trial, when Mrs Terry had to complain of petty acts of larceny. On the 22nd December plaintiff was discharged for dishonesty. In the course of evidence, given by Mrs Terry, she stated that gross perjury had been committed both at that Court and at the Police Station. The plaintiff had no character, and no clothes. His Honour said he had to consider probabilities and determine upon which side the balance was. With the charge of theft he had nothing to do. He gave judgment for 16s 8d [to be paid to Miss Froggatt] and took no notice of the counter claim.

High Peak News, 25 January 1890

WIRKSWORTH

COLLIERS AND I

For a collier boy or young man to be seen with a Parson was certain persecution. It was literally four years before I could say that I felt that I had any hold upon any boy or young man of the collier class. With the 'upper ten' of a colliery village I never could get on.

At last I determined to make a desperate effort to do something for our boys and men. I was also equally determined that whatever I did should be 'of the Church, Churchy' and not be 'Undenominational'. To this determination I faithfully adhered, and how it answered my readers will judge for themselves. In this I knew quite well I should have the entire and hearty support of my Vicar; though I also knew equally well, that whatever I did, if it were to continue and prosper, my dear good Vicar must have no more than a nominal connection with it; and for this reason, that earnestly desirous as he was to do good, the very best for his people, he had no more idea of how to manage a young collier than the said collier would know how to manage him.

In July, 1877, the good man went off for a month! I seized the opportunity, the only one I ever had (poor man, he never made such a mistake again as to leave his curate alone), I seized the opportunity and started 'the Guild of S. Bartholomew', held a special Evensong, and admitted twelve members, a schoolmaster, a butcher, a hairdresser, eight railway men, and myself. We held our first meeting on July 9th, 1877 in the Church Schoolroom.

For the first fourteen months of its existence this guild went on as such Societies mostly do, meeting once a fortnight, in the School; a paper was read, and then there was discussion and friendly talk. This sort of thing was little or no good. Moreover the young colliers were not touched. It was a great deal too respectable, of which disease it would have died, had I not determined to start a Guild-House, open all day to all members, with library, games, etc. When I made up my mind to this, I was living in 'my own hired house' in the village. One memorable day, I invited twelve youths to my house to tea. They were out-and-outers, poor fellows, with great good hearts, but blackguards, pure and simple. I love to think of them now, I can hear their voices, see their sly looks. The tea was enjoyed, and then their tongues began to be let loose. 'Well Mester, tha't a-rum-'un, I ne'er thaut as parsons wor same as yow. If I hear onyboddy a callin' yow I'll feight em, weant we Pem? We'll gee um some fist and ma't claret run fro' their bloody smellers, we will that, mun.' At last the ice was broken. I went next day to an Auctioneer, sold up all my furniture, got a basin full of money, and started my Guild-House, in which the first meeting was held on September 16th, 1878, with eighteen members present.

Of course, first, to the blessing of God I attribute the splendid success of this work, the results of which I can see even to-day after all these years. What was God's blessing upon? It was upon the true affection, and perfect trust we had for each other; there was nothing they would hide from me.

CLAY CROSS COLLIERY

SANDIACRE

Never were the members of any family more bound to one another than we were, never was there more intense grief than when we had to part. For these 'chaps' I simply lived, and for them I would have died, and they knew it. I trusted them and they trusted me.

My readers must not imagine all these youths were saints and angels, sitting quietly and playing 'innocent' games or reading in their Guild-House. They were as full of noise and mischief as ever they could stick, and it was only by heavy fines that they were kept in subjection at all. Yet so devoted were they to their 'Guild,' so much did they appreciate its blessings and benefits, that they would readily pay one shilling and sixpence rather than be expelled. The fines in one year have amounted to as much as seven pounds.

The house consisted of five rooms, and the rent was four and sixpence per week. The downstairs front room was a general room where the members might do pretty much as they liked; here have I sat night after night for hours and hours, talking, teaching, lecturing, and telling tales: this last amusement they were particularly fond of. The front room upstairs was called the 'reading room', though very little reading did they do beyond magazines and comic papers. Another good large room upstairs I kept locked, and used it for myself, for special classes and interviews. Here I may say that I shall always speak of the members of this guild as 'boys', we always called each other 'boys'. None could be members until they were

END OF THE SHIFT, SHIPLEY COLLIERY

confirmed, and the usual age at that time was fifteen to six-teen. Among themselves, they always called me the 'boss,' to my face they called me 'Mr'.

The fines were:
1. For breaking Furniture   3d
2. Swearing   3d
3. Fighting   3d
4. For singing 'Hi Tidili-i-ti'   3d
5. For going to Theatre   6d
6. For going to Public-Houses   1/6

It is worse than futile to imagine that any genuine good can be accomplished in any individual case by merely being a member of an institute or football club. They are very good appendages, but the real work lies in the interviews with each boy. Here the Priest must be perfectly straight in his questions, language, and advice – there must not be the slightest hesita-tion. The language he uses must be taken from the boys' own pit vocabulary, any other is hopeless.

There were, during these years, some races held every year. The company was such, that I made a rule, and stuck to it, that anyone attending them should be expelled, and I find among the records of the guild several names of members so expelled; but eventually they almost always returned in peni-tence, paying a heavy fine. I also laid on a heavy fine for any members going to Chapel. On Ascension Day, 1879, and after till 1888, the members always communicated at 4.30 a.m.; and I have seen as many as seventy pit men and boys at that ser-vice, in their pit clothes, prepared to start off to work when the service was over.

The 'boys' by this time had become so numerous, and were so thoroughly united, that they cared nothing about being styled, as they constantly were, 'Metcalfe's Pups', 'Metcalfe's Greasehorns', 'Old Metcalfe's Imps', 'The Parson's Bodyguard', 'Young Devil-Dodgers', and such like interesting and descriptive names.

On May 1st, 1881, a Confirmation was held in our church, at which a band of youths were confirmed who, with few exceptions, turned out well, and were from that time the backbone of the guild. The Confirmation was in the morning. In the afternoon, I went with the candidates for a little sort of pic-nic on the banks of the pretty little river Amber. We all divested ourselves of our clothes, and set to work to dam up the stream, and make a fortification which some of us were to defend and some attack. In the middle of our fun came a man in a terrible rage, and used red language – for, about half a mile down the stream, he had a mill, which ceased to work when we dammed up the water. Of course, we had to undo our work, and apologise. With difficulty I persuaded him not to summon us. In after years, this man became a good friend, and his boy one of our members.

F.J. Metcalfe (Rector of Killamarsh)

COAL STRIKE

When I was eighteen or nineteen there was a strike at Dronfield Silkstone and considering that two thirds of the

COAL PICKING DURING THE 'LOCK-OUT', CLAY CROSS

people of Coal Aston worked there you can guess it was a stricken village. They had never known such poverty as they knew then for the strike lasted twenty-two weeks.

One day my sister sent for a loaf of bread but there wasn't one to be had in Coal Aston. The shopkeepers had stopped baking it because there was no hope of them ever getting paid. There was no strike pay, no anything, only charity. The colliers used to go to other pits and stand outside with a book. All the workers were supposed to give sixpence and that comprised the strikers' whole income. Often the men would walk ten to fifteen miles for two-and-six or two shillings. We walked to Killamarsh and sometimes were asked to go in the public house where they passed round the hat for us. All the money collected was pooled together and then divided equally between us all.

During that period was the only time in my life I ever had to manage with half a meal. Others however were in a much worse plight. The wolf was not only at the door but inside and sitting on the table. One night I went to see the blacksmith of the Silkstone pit who lived at Coal Aston. What a sorry state of affairs I found!

There were six children and all of them crying, Heaven knows when they had a meal last. The mother was crying also and the husband was sitting in a corner, inert, glum and stupid. I asked if one of them would come with me to see Halifax, the Relieving Officer, and the mother volunteered.

Arrived at the officer's house I explained how they were situated but he said he couldn't do anything and that I knew was

a lie. I never could understand why some people are so loath to part with money that is not their own. If it had been his money I asked him for, I could have understood him, but it wasn't. Much rather did it belong to the poor woman who was with me.

I went away raging inwardly against the niggardly soul of him who had refused assistance to starving children. Something had to be done, so when we were back in the blacksmith's house I asked him, 'Will you come with me?'

He looked up sullenly.

'Where to?' he wanted to know.

Losing all my patience with him, I retorted, 'We shall have to find something to eat for these kids, whether you have anything or not.'

He never answered, he might not have heard, the way he was sitting like a dumb, foolish, obstinate dummy.

At last I asked the mother if she would fetch a Mrs Riggarts whom I knew was also very poor.

She agreed and asked me, 'Where are we going?'

I said, 'We might go to prison before we get back.'

Nothing daunted the two women went with me and I took them to the Relieving Officer's hen roost. Here I caught two fowls, wrung their necks and put them in the women's aprons.

'Take them home,' I said, 'Then come back and meet me by yon stile.'

When they came back we went into the Relieving Officer's field and I filled their aprons with potatoes and a swede each. After I had packed them off home I fetched them bread from

THE RENT MEETING, OCKBROOK

our house. So that night and next morning at least they had a good tuck in at the Relieving Officer's expense, but he never knew it for he never found out.

The men had struck because the new owner of the pit wanted to lower their wages. This they would not agree to and the final result of it was that the owner, Mr Addy, went bankrupt. A Mr Sheard next bought the pit and kept the wages as they were, thus after over twenty weeks of idleness and privation the men went back to work.

Joseph Sharpe

OLD-FASHIONED DERBYSHIRE PUDDING

A batter pudding is made in the usual manner, with four ounces of sieved flour and a pinch of salt put in a bowl, and a well formed in the centre. Into this drop two eggs. Beat in the flour, allowing it to fall from the sides until the eggs and flour are made into a batter. Add slowly half a pint of milk, and a tablespoon of cold water, beating all the time to get rid of lumps. Keep beating until the batter is so light that some bubbles form. Cover with a cloth and leave an hour for the flour to swell. Have ready a pound of gooseberries, picked and washed and fresh. Place a little dripping in a deep meat tin, and make it hot in the oven. Pour in the batter when ready and drop the gooseberries with a little sugar dredged over them into the batter, keeping the fruit separately spaced. Put the tin in the oven and bake for one hour. This pudding is served with sugar, and the sour taste of the gooseberries mingles well with the smooth taste of the batter. It was a cottage pudding, much loved for the ease in cooking it.

On very busy days, such as wash-days when owing to bad weather a lot of washing had accumulated and everyone was too busy to cook, we had a special pudding, called by the title I liked

ALEC LAMB, CODNOR

WEDDING AT BULLBRIDGE

OCKBROOK LODGE PRIVATE DAY SCHOOL

KINGS NEWTON

so much, Hasty Pudding. It was made in five minutes, a simple dish, despised by adults but adored by children, partly for its romantic name, and because we saw it boiling with haste to be ready.

Flour was mixed with cold water to a thick batter. Then spoonfuls were dropped into a large pan of fast-boiling salted water. The flour formed queer shapes, and these shapes were taken from the pan with a large perforated ladle and dropped on hot plates. They were covered with golden syrup and eaten very hot. Nothing could be simpler, and this pudding must have been eaten by primitive man, I thought as I grew older. I could see them grinding the wheat ears in a stone quern such as we had in the garden, boiling spring water over an open fire and dropping the wheaten flour into the water in some kind of an iron pot.

Alison Uttley

IRISH HELP

Most farmers had an Irishman for a month at least during hay harvest. They usually came over from Ireland to help in the Lancashire hay harvest, then they went into Derbyshire and then into Lincolnshire for the corn harvest and potato harvest.

ASHBOURNE

79

BLACKWELL BRIDGE, MELBOURNE

ASHBOURNE

Some Irishmen came to the same farm for years, one man coming over for forty years, and they always brought their own scythes with them. Wages were £1 per week and keep, including drink in the hay field, and usually a bed was fixed up in a loft or barn for them.

Most of them were very good workers and in a big hurry to get the hay in in good weather. One young Irishman of only eighteen had hands one could have used for a pin cushion and he would not have felt it, they were so hard and horny. He said it was with carting and shovelling on the roads in Ireland.

He was a good eater, too. I remember mother sending two big pies in large earthenware dishes for the Irishman, my brother and myself. One was meat and potato and the other I think was apple. We had eaten the meat and potato one and there was a portion of the apple left, so John, the Irishman, said 'Sure, if you'll eat the half of it, I'll eat the other half', so that left two empty dishes to go back. They were very good with hoes, too, having more practice than we did, I suppose.

F.W. Brocklehurst

BANK HOLIDAY, MATLOCK BATH

BAKEWELL MARKET

Prices remained very much the same, with a good calving cow making about £20. About the best cow father ever had was a red one, which he took to Bakewell Market. All the stalls in the market were full and we stood with her on the corner of what was Mr Sims' shop. There were quite a number of dealers who liked to buy a good cow, and we soon had some customers about. The one who first bid at her was a little sharp man with a bowler hat, whose wife went with him everywhere, carrying a little bag of gold sovereigns to pay for any cattle bought. In a very emphatic manner he would keep coming back and saying that was his last bid, then he would walk away, but never quite far enough to let another dealer get in who was waiting in the offing. This continued quite a while and eventually she was sold for £25, which was a very big price at that time. Everything was sold privately in those days, either on the farm or at the market. The market started very early, the cattle stalls usually being filled by 8 a.m. and father was usually home for dinner – the market all over.

F.W. Brocklehurst

ASHBOURNE MARKET

A RAM FIGHT

On Monday, at the Ashborne County Court, James Renshaw, of Mayfield, sued John Haywood for £8 damages by reason of

WELL-DRESSING, TISSINGTON

defendant's ram getting into plaintiff's field and fighting with his ram and killing it. – Defendant denied that it was his ram, but belonged to his son, but admitted being tenant of the field. – His Honour, in giving judgment, held that the ram was the defendants, and that he had not used sufficient care in taking charge of it. Verdict for plaintiff for the £8 claimed.

Derby Mercury, 14 December 1892

TISSINGTON

The festival of well-dressing, or well-flowering, as it is sometimes called, formerly prevailed in different parts of the country, but appears now to be almost exclusively confined to this particular village; though an attempt has of late years been made to revive the custom at Buxton and some other places in Derbyshire. Ascension Day is that annually set apart for the observance of this custom, which is made a time of mutual feasting and rejoicing, and the pleasant exchange of hospitalities. On the occasion the five wells or springs, which are situ-

ated in different parts of the hamlet, are decorated with arches and niches, adorned with mosaics and arabesques, formed of different coloured flowers and evergreens, and inscribed with appropriate Scripture texts. The business of the day is usually commenced by a service at the church, after which the clergyman in his surplice, attended by the village choir, and followed by the entire congregation, walk in procession to the nearest well, when all form in a circle round, a psalm is read, and afterwards a hymn of thanksgiving sung; and the same thing is repeated at each well in succession. Afterwards the bailiff of Sir Henry Fitzherbert announces that the hall is open for all who are willing to partake of the baronet's hospitality, and the remainder of the day is spent in feasting, dancing, and merrymaking.

James Croston

THE 'KINDERSCOUT' LOBSTER SEASON

My next visit to the 'Scout' was made in the early summer of the present year (1880), from Hayfield, a village which has the

TWYFORD FERRY

CALKE ABBEY

KINDER SCOUT

advantage of standing almost in the centre of the wildest scenery in Derbyshire. The first discovery which my inquiries brought to light was that the Kinderscout is regarded as strictly private property, and that it is divided up among numerous holders, almost all of whom are at loggerheads with each other and with the public. The mountain – for one may so speak of it, seeing that it is close upon 2000 feet in height – is one vast moor, intersected with long, broad gulches, and abounding in deep holes, patches of wet moss, and pools of dark water. There are said to be certain public rights of foot-way, but they do not appear to lead to the best points, and even in regard to these there are constant disputes. Moreover, they are hard to find amidst a labyrinth of heath and ferns, and it is not unusual for the gamekeepers to turn strangers back even when they are upon the paths which are supposed to be fairly open to all. The owners of the moor are jealous to the last degree of their rights, and quarrel over the few birds which by some accident are still left as though the cause of empires were at stake. This arises from the foolish way in which the district has been parcelled out among a number of small holders, in patches not much larger than a table-cloth. One man's allotment is actually under two acres in extent, and his only chance of getting a shot is on the days when his neighbours are out shooting, and the grouse are driven over his field. Then he stands waiting for a chance, and if he can manage to bring a bird down on his

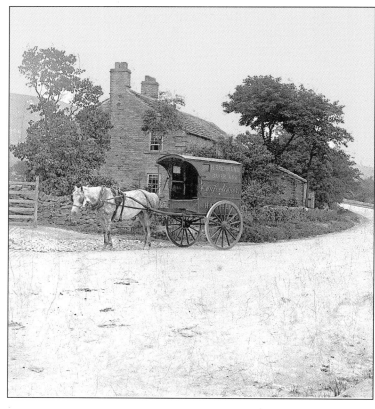

BREAD VAN, HAYFIELD

WILLIAM CLOUGH, HAYFIELD

EYAM

little patch, he has had a fine day's sport, but if the bird drops outside his boundary he goes home with an empty bag. 'But sometimes,' as a keeper informed me, 'you may stand there all day without getting a shot.' On an average during the season there are about three guns out to each bird, and in one case a gentleman who pays £50 a-year for his bit of moor only got two birds all last season – £25 each, and I hope he did not think it too much. When I heard all this, it brought to my mind a line which I had once read in a sort of burlesque almanack – 'August 12th. Lobster shooting begins on the Peak of Derbyshire'. If the Kinderscout is ravaged many years longer as it now is, the 'noble sportsmen' of the district will have as much chance of shooting lobsters there as of finding grouse.

Louis J. Jennings.

THE TALE OF EYAM

The village, deep embosomed in the hills,
Will soon lie hushed in sleep: upon the slope
The lengthening shadow creeps, and gently fills
The meadows with its silence: ample scope
Lurks here for rich imagination's song
Among this fenced group of lichened stone,
The sole mementoes of the peasant dead: these long

To heaven have reared their lettered fronts, o'ergrown
And crusted with their crumbling rinds, now laved
With nightdews and the silken threads of cloud,
That secret spread them o'er these hallowed graves,
Till hill and vale sink wrapped in one vast shroud.
Short space the restless present sleeps its sleep,
Swift let my keener fancy wing its flight,
To usher out the past some memories deep
Of those who perished in a cause of right.
One hundred times, twice told, has winter's snow
Bequeathed its falling mantle to this wold,
Since fiercest scourge of man and direst woe
Bore hence on lightning wing both young and old:
Alike two hundred summer suns have cast
Their evening shades in yonder darkening wood,
Since pestilence, so foul and unsurpassed,
To Eyam's bright homes swept down its hell-born brood.

High rose the wassail, loud the chorused song
That split the midnight air, in darkness spent;
Around they passed the bowl, and tarried long
In tempered jest and harmless merriment:
All friends had met the Wake to celebrate
And dress the wells, but e'er they ceased their mirth
Some spoke of lights in heaven and meteors great,
Some told of wondrous troublings of the earth,
And dark foreboding signs of coming death:
The clustered bees had thrice enswarmed the oak,

86

SWARKESTONE

The lightning reft last spring upon the heath:
The lighter-minded passed it as a joke,
And hurrying through the dancers on the green
To gain secure retreat, they wished their wish,
And lisped their faltering love songs, and unseen
Between their lips they toyed the lingering kiss.
Then mingling in the firelit dance they sped,
And blindly revelled 'neath a thunder-cloud,
That hung its darksome pall above their head,
And hurled from heaven to earth its echoes loud:
Yet one stupendous bolt its fury spent
Upon the fated oak tree, bleached and bare,
With one fell crash its spectral branches rent
And flung the splintered fragments to the air:
As when in haste t' escape the kestrel's swoop
Will little chickens to the mother's wing,
Affrighted and amazed the awe-stricken group
Forsook its sports to gain safe sheltering.
Amid sephulchral voices of the skies
The tongue of Gabriel Hounds perplexed the ear,
With distant bay of dogs and piercing cries,
Like those a dying man will feign to hear.
Oh! terrible that night! and strange presage
Of coming wrath! for e'en the bravest heart
Will quail for fear, when tempests rage
And out heaven's reeking nostrils firebolts start.

Uprose the morning, fresh from un'sturbed sleep,
To light the quivering drops from off the bough,
And furl the rolling vapours up the steep,
And gild with golden sheen the vale below.
Though bright the radiant promise of the morn,
The village brooded at the cottage door;
Alike some mastless vessel, tempest torn,
Floats stunned and sullen when the gale is o'er.
The neighbour friends, who met in last night's feast,
Retraced their footsteps at an early hour,
Soon as the herald rays proclaimed the east:
Yet one there lingered in a sylvan bower,
That dripped its fragrant drops to kiss the ground,
Impatient of the approach of Sydall's lass:
In that retreat last eve had he unwound
His skein of love, what time the blinding flash
Had, spellbound, held her answer in arrest:
With swift appointed meeting had she fled
In instant haste: warm love her cheeks confessed.
As now to grace the bower she upward sped.
Thrice swift the arrow aimed from Cupid's bow,
But swifter still the keener shaft of death,
E'en whiles they dreamed of peace, insatiate foe,
The plague beleaguered with its foulsome breath.
Their prison ope'd the murderous fiends burst forth,
While doubting first men marked the rumour vague,
Until from east to west, from south to north,
Was shrieked that piercing cry, 'The Plague! The Plague!'
The morning saw uprouse her with the lark
The mother hale and hearty from her rest,
The evening closed upon a festering mark,

THE WINNATS, CASTLETON

GRINDLEFORD

That showed the gnawing canker on her breast.
Home came the father down the village street,
Expectant of fond welcome at return,
No loving hand met his, no voice to greet,
Perhaps the morrow's break might bring his turn.
The snooded maid that in the cornfields gleaned,
The lad who brooked no care to crease his brow,
Time honoured age and infancy unweaned
Alike sank victims to the shades below.
But why, when menaced with so cruel end,
Did they not fly? not weakness combat strength:
Nay! why did dauntless band of Spartan men
Thus court destruction at the broadsword's length?
Stern duty to the land he loved so well
Incited each the treacherous risk to try,
Preferring death than men should after tell
And point at him who acted cowardly.
No bells inchimed the Sabbath's sacred morn,
Nor roused soft echoes from the distant hills,
No longer was the weed-patched church-path worn
By tread of feet, but all lay strangely still:
Yet when the rustled leaves refrained to shake,
At times the ear might catch a portioned hymn,

CRATCLIFFE ROCKS, BIRCHOVER

Like faint-heard strains across a moonlit lake,
That come and go behind some island gem.
On Cucklett-dell Mompesson laid his choice,
So lone you e'en might hear the harebell stir,
Round fern-draped rock and cavern rang his voice,
And hushed in solemn awe each listener.
Among that plague-thinned group sat two alone,
Well had they learnt to love those echoes wide,
Brave Roland he of Stoney Middleton,
And she the Sydall's lass, his promised bride.
Each much longed day of rest left he his home,
To cross the bounding line 'twixt life and death,
And willing braved, that they in love might roam,
The pestilence that hung in every breath.
Oft brimmed her eyes with tears as she beseeched
For others' sakes that he'd not come again,
Nor heeded he until Mompesson preached
'The nobler deed is that which gives us pain.'
That night, whilst parting at the boundary well,
Which drew its sparkling water from the stream,
E'en as they touched their hands, a deepened knell
From some old village belfry seemed for them.
What passioned words could mete, or colour paint
The mute despair outsprung from that chance dirge?
As in a dream one helpless hangs and faint
Above a yawning chasm, at its verge
In mid-air dangling from a sapling's bough,

As root by root one feels it tear away,
Yet from the parched throat can wring no sound,
They speechless parted on their downward way.
Four times the moon had waned when next he trod
Within the censured bounds, pale death had gone;
Few had he left to proffer thanks to God
For safe deliverance: too oft peeped the stone,
That marked a resting-place, from tangled grass,
For full three hundred brave and fair lay dead;
But o'er this desolation let me pass
In seeming silence, all looms dark and dread.
The wind is whistling through the creviced wall,
The raindrops patter on my crumpled page,
Long may these stones be left, sad proof to all
Of how our brave men died in that past age.

'An Old Blue'

KEEPER'S GIBBET

Here by a gate-side on a fir-tree's bough, which has suffered from the fury of a storm, some keeper had made his gibbet, displaying the mouldering, mummied carcases of five weasels, hanged ignominiously by the neck till they were dead. By

IRONGATE, DERBY

their side dangled a hawk and other birds of prey which I was not naturalist enough to distinguish. On the ground were the fallen feathers of other malefactors, an unsightly wing or two, and a few bleaching bones. One wonders if these gibbets are efficacious. Are the live weasels frightened to repentance as they look on their dead fellows? Do the timid victims of these ferocious little beasts come here in the gloaming and rejoice at the power which has beaten down the proud and tyrannous? Are these warning examples spoken of in the talk of the bird world and the forest people? Are there wise creatures, Nestors and Mentors of their kind, who draw morals for the behoof of inexperienced youth? Who shall say?

J.B. Firth

THE WIDENING OF SADLER GATE

Sir – Most generations have benefited greatly by the example of the good and great of former times. I trust I am no exception to this. The late Mr John Davis, optician, of Derby, was very much respected. Seeing that the town did not move to widen Iron-gate, then in one place narrower than Sadler-gate, he started a subscription to assist the public funds. The result

was the street was widened. We also owe to him the planting of our streets with trees. Following his example I started a subscription for the removal of the Rotton-row block from our Market-place. The sum subscribed was £5,000 and I had the honour of removing the first tile when the demolition commenced. About thirty years ago some leading townsmen had a scheme for widening Sadler-gate. As action has not been taken, I am wishful to start a subscription to assist in bearing the expense of this very much needed improvement, and having been requested, am willing to act as hon. sec., *pro. tem.*, to a committee for this purpose. Like my father, I have tried to help many good movements; and being now sixty, this may be the last thing in which I may endeavour to benefit my native town. Following the excellent lead of Mr Charles Bakewell, the able and respected chairman of the late committee for removing Rotton-row block, I propose that subscriptions may be divided into four amounts, extending over four years. The Rotton-row matter had excellent support from the Press. I trust this will have. A subscription list is now opened at the Derby and Derbyshire Bank. –

Yours sincerely,
Henry Steer, F.R.Hist.S.
1, Iron-gate, Derby.

Derby Mercury, 26 October 1891

MIDLAND RAILWAY STATION, DERBY

THE MIDLAND RAILWAY WORKS

The proverbial play of 'Hamlet' with the part of Hamlet omitted would be really a somewhat complete performance compared to Derby without the Midland Railway Company. In fact, the Midland Railway Company *is* Derby, and it would be difficult to imagine the town as other than the centre of this colossal railway system. Without the Midland, Derby would be a dreamy old-world town, where Rip Van Winkle might sleep undisturbed. It would be about as big as Ashbourne, and as animated as Ashby-de-la-Zouch. If the Midland Company were to remove their head-quarters, if they were to take their great workshops and foundries and offices elsewhere, Derby would become at once a place preposterously large for its population. The inhabitants would flee from the town as from a city condemned to destruction. *Ichabod!* would be written on the walls. The streets would be silent, deserted, grass-grown. In describing Derby, the chronicler would experience the cheerful feelings of Marius surveying the ruins of Carthage, or of Macaulay's New Zealander, seated on a broken arch of London Bridge, sketching the ruins of St Paul's.

Employing something like ten thousand of the population of Derby, directly at its own works and offices, with work that is not subject to the trade fluctuations of other pursuits, and indirectly engaging the contractors and ironfounders and other tradesmen of

the town, it will at once be seen what an important relation the Midland Railway sustains to local industries. It was almost by a fluke that the Midland made Derby its head-quarters. Nottingham was the town chosen for the honour; but the municipal Dogberrys of the town of lace and 'lambs' rejected the railway advances. Nottingham's loss has been Derby's gain. Derby itself was not, however, very enthusiastic over the new enterprize; and it almost puts one out of temper with one's ancestors to think of the narrow escape the town had of missing the incomparable commercial advantages it now enjoys by being the centre of so vast a system.

Derby station, with its vast area of prolonged platforms, and its bustling life, may be thought a large place; but it is not, according to the local mind, the 'station' at all. The 'station,' according to the Derby acceptation of the term, is comprised in the blocks of business offices where the management of the Midland system is conducted; in the mighty congeries of workshops, flaming with forge-flares, and noisy with ringing hammers: where tools of every denomination operate upon metal of every kind; where locomotives that are miracles of mechanism, are fashioned by Titans of toil, like the monster of Frankenstein's; where carriages and wagons are constructed, from the drawing-room on wheels to the rude coal truck, telegraphs made, and signals erected. These works occupy an astonishing area of ground. The Locomotive Department, which is the most interesting, is situated

91

LOCOMOTIVE DEPOT, DERBY

REFRESHMENTS, DERBY STATION

ILKESTON

at the back of the passenger station; the Signal works are by the side of the Derwent at the north end; the Telegraph shops are at the south end of the platforms; and the Carriage and Wagon Department lies at the south-west extremity, adjoining Osmaston Park, and in immediate proximity to the site of the Royal Agricultural Show. A visit to these workshops is a liberal education.

Edward Bradbury and Richard Keene

Derby County v. Oxford University

A strong team of the County met Oxford University on Wednesday on the County Ground. The visitors were late in turning up, and the game was started nearly twenty-five minutes late. The only absentee on the home side was A. Goodall, whose instep is slightly injured. His place was taken by Leiper, and, winning the toss, J. Goodall decided to play towards the town in the first half. Oxford kicked off, but the County getting possession had much the best of matters and Mills, after the ball had been passed and repassed in front of the visitor's goal, put in a splendid centre, Bloomer missing an easy chance. J. Goodall and Mills each missed opportunities of scoring, and then the 'Varsity temporarily attacked; but the ball never reached the home custodian. Staley cleared, and the Oxford goal was again strongly attacked. Two corners were forced, but proved of no advantage. Raikes twice saved warm shots from Leiper. After successfully defending for 15

STANTON-BY-DALE

DUFFIELD

minutes Goodall beat the backs, and scored a pretty goal. Kicking off the visitors got away, Salt, by plucky play, getting in a good position but shooting over. The game soon settled down again at the opposite end, the ball being transferred by a fine run by Little, and Bloomer very shortly added a second. Give and take play followed, the Varsity team putting in some fast and good play. Soon, however, the visitorss were again forced to keep on the defence of the goal, the home forwards swarming round the goal, innumerable shots going anywhere but between. Very seldom the County allowed their opponents to reach the halfway line, and the interval arrived without Robinson having had to handle a shot, although just before the whistle blew the visitors gained a corner. Half-time:–

Derby County 2
Oxford 0

The second half opened with an attack by the County, and Oxford twice ran the ball over the line, and then a fruitless corner to the County followed, and Robinson had to save two easy shots in the next few minutes, the visitors quite holding their own, and Goodall got away nicely and passed to Bloomer, who shot straight at Raikes, who saved. The Varsity right ran down finely, and, passing to Smith, that player put in a really splendid shot, which Robinson had no chance of saving. Encouraged by their success,

the visitors played up well, and twice shots just grazed the uprights. Continuing to play with more vigour, the visitors pressed for a time, but eventually the County woke up, and the forwards going away in a line Little added a third. After this the home side had again the best of the game. Robinson with a bit of luck, twice stopped shots from close quarters, and was obliged to give a corner, which was of no advantage. Darkness was now coming on, with a quarter of an hour to play. Each side pressed in turn, the Oxford backs putting in some very fine kicking and defending well. Mills forced another unproductive corner. The remainder of the game, which was played in semi-darkness, was all in favour of the County, excepting the last few minutes, during which the visitors gained two corners, which, however, were easily saved. Final result –

County 3
Oxford 1

The teams were:–

Derby County:– W. Robinson, goal; W. Methven and J. Staley, backs; E. Hickinbottom, J. Leiper, and W. Roulston, half-backs; S. Mills and S. Bloomer, right wing; J. Goodall, centre; J. Little and J. McMillan, left wing.

Oxford University:– G.B. Raikes, goal; W.J. Oakley and O.B. Fry, backs; T.C. Robinson, E.C. Bliss, and E.B. Alexander, half-

94

BRADBOURNE

backs; R.J. Salt and C.B. Hewitt, right wing; G.O. Smith, centre; B. Street and J. Walker, left wing.

Referee – Mr P.G. Exham, Repton School.

Linesman – (Derby County) Mr Holloway.

Derby Mercury, 28 December, 1892

LUNCH FOR THE ANGLER

This day I fished alone up the Dale. Our hostess sent my lunch up to me by Jack, our boy. He came mounted on a big white donkey, and in front of him was Master three-year-old Bobby; Miss Daisy, a bright, dark-eyed girl of ten, came with them. They found me plying my avocation at the feet of the 'Twelve Apostles'. These grand, lichen-mantled, steeple-like rocks stand as guardians at the entrance of the Dale, brow-beaten, as it were, by an enormous projecting rock on the opposite side of the river, from the top of which a despairing lover (or perhaps a desparing pair of them) is said to have leaped and buried his or their sorrows in the waters below – hence the rock is called the Lover's Leap.

Daisy soon disappeared, scrambling up the rocky sides like a young gazelle, up and up amongst the hazel bushes, where, as she well knew, huts were plentifully hidden up behind the inaccessible rocks.

No sooner had she disappeared than I, making a long cast over a rising fish, hung my fly on the topmost branch of a young hawthorn bush away up among the rocks. I sent Jack up to get the fly, and so I was left alone with the baby. He was sitting sturdily on the donkey, holding the reins tight, and presently he managed to pull his head round towards home while I was adjusting my fly. I did not see the start, but Bobby was shouting 'Dee-up, donkey!' and working his little legs on the donkey's side, and off the donkey went at a brisk walk.

As soon as I saw them, I walked as quietly and as fast as I could, so as not to start him off, but as I got up just near enough to put my hand on the bridle, off he bolted full gallop, Master Bobby clinging like a little man to his neck; he soon came tumbling down, to my no small alarm. Luckily he fell easily on the soft grass. After a jolly good roar, he was for a time pacified, but when he saw the donkey disappearing round the rocky corner he set up another hullaballoo, and I could do nothing to pacify him. There were a dozen excursionists on the other side who witnessed the whole of the

SMEDLEY'S HYDRO, MATLOCK

tragedy, evidently with much amusement. I shouted for Jack till I was hoarse, but in vain: no Jack appeared for a long time. He eventually came along, quite alarmed when he saw that the donkey had disappeared.

He said that somehow he had lost his way and couldn't get down nohow. I said, 'You young scamp, you've been nutting.' This he stoutly denied, but as I heard him cracking nuts all the evening afterwards I was obliged to doubt the truth of his assertion. Daisy turned up soon with bag full of nuts, and as the donkey couldn't get through the iron gate, and was not fool enough to try to get over it, nor yet to swim across the river, he was soon captured. Bobby and Daisy and donkey started for home, and reached it without further disaster.

'The Amateur Angler'

DAMAGE BY LIGHTNING IN DERBYSHIRE

A storm of terrible severity raged in the Peak of Derbyshire on Wednesday. The heavy downpour of rain was attended by fearfully vivid forked and sheet lightning, while the thunder claps were deafening. Damage was done to the Midland Railway telegraphic service at Monsal Dale, and the Buxton

THE CONSERVATORY, SMEDLEY'S HYDRO

MACKWORTH

telegraphic connection with the Hope Valley circuit is entirely disconnected, owing to the lightning having fused the coils and protectors.

The storm of Wednesday night did a good deal of damage in East Derbyshire, a mare and foal, belonging to Mr J.B. Barrow, Ringwood Hall, were grazing in a field on the Ringwood Farm, when they were struck by the electric fluid and killed. The loss is estimated at not less than £60. About ten o'clock, a house at New Brimington, occupied by Mr Ebeneser Whitworth, was struck by the electric fluid and much damaged. A young man named Fuller, a lodger, was injured about the shoulders and arms, and rendered quite helpless. Later in the evening he had a fit, and has continued in a serious condition. At Eckington the Miners' Arms beer-house in Pit-street, was struck by the electric fluid, damaging the roof and gable end. The inmates were much alarmed, but escaped unhurt. Two houses, in the occupation of Burwell Crookes and Frederick Bingham, and situate on Hill Top Common, Dronfield, were struck. The lightning appears to have entered Crookes' house through the tiles to two bedrooms below, in one of which two children were in bed. Mrs Crookes had just gone up to fetch them down. Fortunately neither the mother nor children were hurt, though much frightened. From walls and ceilings of these two rooms the

paper and plaster was torn away. In the back room on the ground floor the greatest damage was done. Here the walls in all directions were denuded of paper and plaster. On the wall were hanging several pictures, which were all torn from the walls, and the glass shivered into thousands of pieces. In the house of Mr Bingham the lightning appears to have entered by the window, and has considerably damaged the walls. A house at Coalaston, in the occupation of Edward Unwin, was also struck.

The thunderstorm of Thursday evening, which broke over Derby shortly after five o'clock accompanied by heavy rain, was the severest which has been experienced in this district for many years. The lightning was very vivid and the thunder had a peculiar low rumbling, which gradually burst into heavier claps. The storm lasted exactly ninety minutes, and some idea of its severity may be obtained when we state that the fall of the rain registered by Mesers John Davis and Son, of Ames Alley was 1.88 [in], due to the actual storm and 1.98 for the whole day. The last heavy rainfall was on June the 4th, which measured 1.58 for the 24 hours.

Great inconvenience and some damage was done by the rush of water. The culvert which runs across the valley between Burton-road and Uttoxeter-road, parallel with Boyer-street, over-flowed, and the adjoining thoroughfares were

LITTLE EATON

quickly converted into running streams of water, some inches deep. Two outhouses in the neighbourhood were washed down, and one person assures us that the storm was so violent that he saw a little dog washed along the street.

At Quarndon the thunderstorm of Thursday was experienced in great severity. It seemed to centre itself over the lower part of the village. It will long be remembered by the inhabitants, young and old. Commencing at five o'clock it lasted until half past six, the lightning, both fork and sheet, being the whole time terrific incessant – in fact, there was scarcely any intermission between the flashes; while the crashes of thunder were loud and continuous. A perfect deluge of rain fell, the water rushing down Quarn Hill in torrents and flooding many places.

Many cattle, sheep, &c., were destroyed in the storm, and a number of farmers sustained very severe losses. At Darley Abbey several sheep and cows were killed.

The thunderstorm on Thursday evening was very severe at Ashborne. There was an exceedingly heavy downpour of rain, and in several parts of the town water flooded the basement floors of many dwellings, through the sewers being unable to take the unusual flood of water. Happily there are no reports to hand of any serious accidents.

At Bakewell the storm lasted upwards of two hours, the thunder was exceptionally loud and the lightning frequent and vivid. A singular accident is reported from Flagg. Three men were sitting in the house of a man named Hodgkinson, when the lightning struck the chimney, doing considerable damage. None of the men were hurt, but a dog, which was lying under a sofa in the same room, was killed on the spot. On Wednesday night a valuable brood mare, belonging to the landlord of the Newhaven Hotel, was struck, and though injured considerably it is believed will recover.

In the district of Melbourne the thunderstorm lasted about three hours. Four young beasts belonging to Mr Bently, St Bride's Farm, were killed by the electric fluid, they were at the time in a shed or barn. An oak tree near to Hawthorne House was also struck, while the heavy rain caused the brook that feeds the pool to very rapidly overflow its banks, doing very considerable damage to a large number of allotment garden plots on its bank.

Derby Mercury, 1 July, 1891

PIKELETS AND OATCAKES

Pikelets were the delicious thin companions of the oatcakes, the stable dish instead of bread a hundred years ago. No bread was baked when wheat was so dear at the time of the Corn Laws, and every farmer could grow oats on the poor rocky soil. So great batches of oatcakes were made each week and hung up to dry like brown washing on a line. We adored oatcakes but they were never

THE 'BIRD CAGE', MELBOURNE HALL

ICE-CREAM SELLER, HOLYMOOR

made at home, for the oatcake man came every fortnight, walking across the hills on mountain paths with his large basket of oatcakes on his arm. He also sold pikelets, which we bought. Oatcakes were toasted and eaten with dripping, pikelets had butter and this was the rule.

Pikelets

Half an ounce of yeast (this was also sold by the oatcake man, and we bought a little each time he visited us), some flour and a quart of milk, a cupful of melted butter and a little salt are needed. Make the milk warm on the top of the stove and stir into it the yeast. This heating of the yeast is important, for the heat has to be low, and a saucepan should not be used. Instead the milk should be put in an enamel or metal bowl to get slightly warm. Then add sufficient flour to make it into a batter. Set it on the hearthstone to rise before the fire for an hour, and shield from draughts. Then add the butter melted. Stir it well. Pour it into iron rings previously placed on a hot plate or griddle, and bake very lightly on both sides. The colour should be pale gold. It takes five minutes to cook after the top has blistered with bubbles. Leave to cool and dry. Then toast and butter well when hot.

Alison Uttley

BOLSOVER CASTLE

I found myself in an ancient hall, vaulted, with stone pillars, and mouldering portraits on the walls of men and women who lived and died three hundred years ago. Everything was very old – the wainscoting, the windows, the furniture which looked as if it might have been there from a time almost forgotten. A date upon a cabinet made it appear far more modern than its apparent age, for it went back only to 1535. Then I passed into another vaulted room, with a large stone pillar in the middle, and into a third with a stone ceiling and black panellings, and through an ancient door which opened upon the broad wall outside. From thence the view around was superb, but the winds raved and roared so violently that it was distressing to stand there. 'It is always terrible windy here,' said the old woman, 'and sometimes you cannot hear the sound of your own voice.' The voices of the winds drowned everything – loud, angry, menacing: it was as if the guardian spirits of the place were wroth at the presence of a stranger.

Then we came to the Star-room, with a ceiling in faded blue and gold, and a beautiful marble mantelpiece. There, too, was an old chair, originally in white and gold, but now much decayed, in which Bess of Hardwicke used to sit – for this part

100

BOLSOVER CASTLE

of Bolsover was built by her, upon the cellars and foundations of a Norman castle. There was an aspect about all these rooms which I have never seen elsewhere, and which I cannot describe. 'It looks like a haunted house,' said I to the woman. 'You would say so if you lived here,' she replied, but at that moment she said no more.

She opened a little door and remarked, 'This bedroom is called Hell.' Truly an uncommon name for a bedroom, but it was an uncommon room, with somewhat mutilated paintings on the ceiling and walls. Whether these are good or bad I cannot say – the day was heavy, and the light but dim, and patches were off the paintings as if they had been scraped. A dreary little room is this, notwithstanding the 'pictures' and the beautiful little fireplace in the corner – a room in which if one ventured to lie down at night spectral shapes would perhaps come in at yonder ancient door, and unearthly voices would cry out 'Sleep no more'. 'Very strange noises are heard here at night,' said the old woman, 'but we do not mind them. They are heard all over the house.' Then to another room called the 'Duke's Chamber' – what Duke I know not, but he must have lived ages ago. Then to another bedroom called 'Heaven'.

We ascended many stone steps, and came to the upper bedrooms, where the shutters are just as they were made, panellings and carvings all untouched. Then we saw dark recesses in the tower, some of them with grated windows through which a very little light struggled, and which the woman said were dungeons. One of them is called 'Mary Queen of Scots' dungeon, for in this weird house, too, was poor Mary a prisoner. Then out upon the leads at the top of the castle, where there is a wondrous view, which at another time I might have dwelt long upon, but the wind shrieked and blustered, and my mind was full of the mystery of the old house.

As I passed back through the rooms they filled me with a feeling which I cannot explain. It may seem that I am drawing an over-coloured picture, or taking a page from Mrs Radcliffe's novels; but it is not so. I truly describe what I saw, and how it impressed me. It may be that the place would not make the same impression upon another person; it may even be that when the sky is blue and the sun is shining into the rooms, the house may wear a smiling, perhaps a commonplace, aspect. I cannot say. I only know that from the moment the outer door was closed an influence which I have never felt within any walls before came over me, and comes back perfectly clear and fresh to my recollection whenever I think of Bolsover Castle.

It is a sombre and ghostly house, and I had got far on my way to Chesterfield before I had shaken its influences entirely from my spirit.

Louis J. Jennings

101

BOOTH FARM, KINDER

A WALK ON KINDERSCOUT

If the Kinderscout range were in Switzerland, scores of books would have been written about it, and 'Sanatoria' without number would have been established on its hill-sides. As it is, not a dozen tourists thoroughly explore the Peak in the course of as many years, and the very people at the local inns which are nearest to it – and they are all some miles distant – seem to know little or nothing about it.

I kept on the brow of the hill, on the Edale side, for some little distance, reluctant to descend. Then I scrambled down, with a careful eye for the 'cloughs,' which are rather steep hereabouts, in the direction of a farmhouse to the north-west. A cart lane runs from this house to the main road, and goes meandering along to two or three cottages which are known as the village of Barber Booth. Here I crossed a little bridge, and turned sharp to the right, westward, and pursued my way till I reached another small village called Upper Booth. There is nothing whatever to tempt the stranger to linger at either of these villages. An old woman told me to go on till I came to 'Measter Shirt's fëarm', and this I did, finding that at Mr Shirt's gates the road came to an end, for the valley now ended also,

being entirely closed up by a hill or mountain of some 1800 feet in height. A wilder or more romantic spot the heart of man could not desire. Master Shirt's farm had a very comfortable and home-like appearance, and as it stood to all appearance on the very borders of civilization, the wilderness beginning just beyond, I determined to see if it were possible to obtain a glass of milk, there being no chance of arriving at another house for many a mile to come. As it turned out, it was fully five hours before I again saw the dwelling-place of man. The good farmer's wife received me very kindly, and I sat down in her old-fashioned parlour, and had a chat with her and two young ladies, while four children stood looking at me, in evident doubt as to whether I belonged to their tribe or not. The ladies told me that a stranger seldom passed that way, and that the only person they saw there besides the members of their own family was the postman. He trudges through the Edale valley from one end to the other every day, winter and summer; and although his berth is not an easy one, especially when the snow is three feet upon the ground, I would much rather have it than live in a city where one is poisoned with fog and smoke, and is obliged every day to gulp down 'blacks' as big as a cheese-plate.

THE SHEEP WASH, KINDER

I now made some enquiries as to the Kinderscout, and was told that there would be objections to my going over the hill to it, for the 'shooters' were out. This was bad news, but I found that there was a path round the hill, which took one fairly into the Kinderscout region, and from thence on to Hayfield. Perhaps, too, I could get across the moors to Chapel-en-le-Frith, which would suit me better than Hayfield, since I was to sleep at Castleton again that night. One of the young ladies then informed me that she had never yet been up the hill near the house, tempting as it looked. With the gallantry which I trust will ever distinguish me, I at once offered to conduct her up the perilous way, and down again if necessary, but unfortunately domestic circumstances prevented her accepting this proposal. Having now drunk up the milk, I clapped on all sail once more, and followed a rough cart-track which had been pointed out to me, and which led upwards over a picturesque bridge across a mountain torrent, through most charming scenery, the glorious hills extending far and wide, all covered with heath in full bloom, and a brawling brook running down at the foot of them straight through the green smiling valley of Edale. The mass of rocks in front are on the Kinderscout itself – the 'Joseph Rocks' – and to the right of them there is another vast pile, like the ruins of some old castle, dismantled by a heavy bombardment. The painter or sketcher may well wish to linger long in this lovely spot. On rounding the top of the

REBEKAH MARRIOTT, KINDER

MELBOURNE HALL

hill, a sea of mountains suddenly appears, not so high as Mont Blanc it is true, but very beautiful in form, and grouped together in a way which delights the eye and impresses the imagination far beyond the power of words to describe. It is not, after all, the height of a mountain which alone makes it beautiful, so much as its situation and surroundings. If we are to talk of mere 'bigness,' Mont Blanc itself is a mere baby compared with Mount Everest in the Himalayas. The grouping and surroundings of these Derbyshire hills are so charming that they linger in the memory long after much grander scenes are forgotten.

Louis J. Jennings

SKATING AT MELBOURNE

The ice on the large pool bore splendidly on Boxing Day, and the continous frost has since then added to it, till now it is some 7^1/$_2$ inches thick. Needless to say great numbers have disported themselves thereon. On Friday a scheme for sweeping the ice was promulgated, and several residents on the margin of the pool placed subscriptions in the hands of Mr A.S. Jacques for this purpose. Several skaters also contributed, and so six brooms were set at

once to work, and by Saturday afternoon a large area was swept and improved. It would be a good thing if schemes of this character were more generally adopted, and if the skating public were prepared to subscribe generally some working men, now out of work, might have the means of earning a few shillings, whilst at the same time the enjoyment of skaters might be considerably enhanced.

Derby Mercury, 4 January 1893

UPLAND FARMING

Most of the farms were very small in those days, from fifty to seventy acres, and money was very scarce. Cheese making was the main source of income. This started about mid-April, and usually two farmers joined so as to make bigger cheeses. The cheese was made in a big pan holding about forty gallons and the one who was not making took his milk evening and morning to his partner, and the milk was measured in a gallon can, then a pint, and a tally was kept of how much one owed or was owed. The cows were all milked in the fields by hand all summer, sometimes the milk being carried on yokes with perhaps another can held in front, for almost a mile. Some of

THORPE CLOUD AND ILAM

the milk was heated on the fire to bring it all up to a certain temperature, and rennet, or part of a calf's stomach, would be added, the pan covered up and left to turn. When the milk had turned into curd, mother would first use her arm and then a wooden bowl to break it down and divide the whey from the curd, which was then pressed to the bottom of the pan and the whey taken off. The curd was then cut up, put into a cloth and then under a small press to clean it of more whey. After dinner it was taken out, put in a pancheon and then crimmed, or worked with the hands, while salt was added and thoroughly mixed in. It was then put into a cheese vat, with a tin garth fitted inside that could go down as weight was added, and it was then put under a large press consisting of a very large square stone fitted on to a screw and fixed in a frame. After a day or two in this, it was taken out and put into a drying room. Even in those days there was much foreign competition and I remember father being away all day with a load of cheese in the cart and coming back without selling any. I believe the highest price offered was 4*d* per lb.

When cheese making was finished, about September, any milk from cows was either used for butter, being 'set-up' as we called it, in pancheons on the pantry bench, and the separated milk being used to feed pigs or calves. All calves born were kept to about one month old, and were given up to two gallons of milk per day, so making them into good veal. Cows were kept milking as long as they would without feeding corn or extra concentrates, then they were dried off for perhaps three months before calving began. Work would consist of milking and giving a feed of hay to the cows and young stock, suckling calves, feeding pigs and any hens close to the farm; after breakfast feeding the rest of the hens, turning the cows and stirks (young heifers) out to water while they were cleaned out, and then perhaps manure carting if frosty or dry, and ploughing if mild. Then there was hay to get in every few days, walling or building gaps that had fallen, and cleaning hen cotes out.

We usually kept a few sheep, selling most of the lambs, but keeping a few ewe lambs to keep up the flock. Everyone kept Lincoln Long Woos in those days, and I remember later on cutting twenty seven lbs of wool from a tup, the ewes averaging fourteen lbs a fleece. Every spring my cousins and I, whose father farmed in the village, would go round the small flocks and try to count the lambs before they arrived, and there was great disappointment if they did not come up to expectations, and drastic action threatened.

105

BASLOW

Most of the cattle were Shorthorns of various colours and milking was all done by hand. Not much recording was done, and in buying a bull one never knew if his parents had good milking blood in their veins, or were beef Shorthorns. A lot of diseases that can be cured easily now, or prevented, were very serious then, such as milk fever, abortion and black leg. There was no getting rid of tuberculous cows and forming attested herds. Milk fever, which is now one of the easiest things to cure, was often fatal then. I remember father and uncle going to sit up all night with a cow of grandfather's. I do not know if the vet had given it up or what, but they had given it half a bottle of whisky, and piled hay on it and rugs, to get a sweat, and the cow got better. They used to be great believers in hot beer and whisky for all sorts of chills and they were probably not far wrong, but it would be rather more expensive now. Father always got some black treacle ready for a cow calving, and as soon as she calved he gave her some scalded maize meal or oatmeal with half a pound of black treacle, made up to two or three gallons.

We usually kept a sow or two and fattened one up to kill in the autumn after perhaps two litters. Feeding was usually maize meal and bran, so that the back fat was about five inches thick and went down a long way before there was any sign of lean. I don't think it would go down very well these days. It was quite an event when the pig was killed. There was a professional pig killer in the village who would come down about 2 p.m. and with extra help to hold it, the pig was duly killed and some blood caught to make black puddings. In the mean-

time water had been boiled to scald the bristles off; afterwards it was hung up, and all the liver, kidneys, heart etc, taken out and divided up to send round to relations, who would in turn send us some when they had killed a pig. The pork would also be taken out and divided up in the same way, keeping the biggest portion for ourselves. The pig killer was a big, tall, very quiet man, very methodical in his ways, and it was usually about 4.30 p.m. when he had finished and, of course, was duly invited in to tea. Next day he would come to cut the pig up, and it was then put in salt with brown sugar and salt petre added. It was usually rubbed till moist so that the salt would penetrate better. The charge for killing and cutting up was 2s 6d, quite a nice side-line in those days. Although the pig killer was very quiet, his wife was a great talker, and when remonstrated with by her husband she said, 'Well, I can talk, can't I?', and he replied, 'Tha can, and prattily'.

When I was nine or ten years of age, we started keeping more poultry. Father bought boxes which were taken to pieces and hen-cotes made out of them, usually six feet by four feet, or we bought cotes with lean-to roofs, for one pound each – twenty hens in each. These were placed in corners of fields so that they got the most shelter from the winds under the stone walls. Only one cote was placed in a two or three acre field, so that the hens could balance their own rations, as they were fed almost entirely on whole maize and a few of our own oats. We used to go, my sister and I and later my brother, to feed them before school, carrying the corn over half a mile in sacks on our backs, up hill most of the way. Sometimes in winter we

YOULGRAVE

could scarcely get for snow, and the cotes were about covered. The birds were chiefly Plymouth Rock, Blue Andalusians, Leghorns and Wyandottes. Several of the farmers would send away for a sitting of eggs every year and if they turned out good, the other farmers would purchase a cockerel to cross with them. We usually crossed alternate Light and Heavy and, though we got a variety of colours in the pullets, we got quite good results. We used to look in the cotes in the morning to see which hens were laying and if we saw any on the nest for several mornings in succession, we would save them for breeding. We kept strict accounts and we found that they paid 5*s* per bird profit without charging for labour, wages at that time being one pound per week for a good man.

F.W. Brocklehurst

QUIET, QUAINT ASHBOURNE

The distance by road from Derby to Ashbourne is something like a dozen miles. By rail it is only 32 miles. An additional inducement in favour of this route is that the train stops at every way-side station, so that the guard may have a gossip with the station-master; you change at a misanthropical place called Uttoxeter Junction, and wait while the stoker has his hair cut; and you wait again at a one-horse sort of spot named

ASHBOURNE

BRADBOURNE POST OFFICE

SHROVE-TIDE FOOTBALL, ASHBOURNE

Rocester, to (as it seems) allow the engine-driver time to enjoy a pipe of tobacco. If your patience is proof against this *in circumbendibus* line of the North Staffordshire Snailway, there are views during the ride to reward your endurance. The rails run past Tutbury, with its historic castle walls reposing among the deep woods of a commanding hill, and follow the valley of the Dove, giving poets' inspirations of wood and water that make you even wish that the sluggish train would go slower than it does, so that you may mentally adjust the camera of the brain and photograph these 'beauty-spots'. There is some talk of carrying the line on to Dove Dale. I hope the projectors of so sinful a scheme will come to a bad end. Why should the romance of Dove Dale be so chased away? Commerce certainly does not demand the sacrifice, and Pleasure can certainly walk the four picturesque miles that separate the enchantment of Dove Dale from 'the shriek of civilization'. In the third place, you can make Buxton your starting point, and a pleasant pilgrimage it is to Hartington, and thence down the Dale, walking with and not against the river. The scenery fronts you; the rocks then have, as it were, their faces to you; and, as the author of *Lorna Doone* in one of his gentle stories says, 'It is surely more genial and pleasant to behold the river, growing and thriving as we go on, strengthening its voice and enlarging its bosom, and sparkling through each successive meadow with richer plentitude of silver than to trace it against

TWO DALES

its own grain and good-will towards weakness, and littleness, and immature conceptions.'

At the present moment I am at Ashbourne, and, when my friend the Senior (Wr)angler has returned from a certain fishing-tackle maker's, we are going back to Dove Dale. Quiet, quaint, Ashbourne, with its ripple of river, and gables of grey and brown, and glimpses of green tree and filmy smoke. There is an old-world atmosphere in the little town. It is soothing, not striking. The repose of the Middle Ages rests upon its still, silent, shadowy streets. The dreams of dead centuries seem to dwell in the old-fashioned houses. There is a pleasant diversity about the architecture; even the public-houses are ancient and picturesque. Most towns grow newer as they grow older, but Ashbourne is as ancient and peaceful now as it was before Prince Charlie was proclaimed King of England in the Market Place in '45. There are the shadowy nooks and corners of old; the place seems like a dream, a tradition, an antiquity, a moss-grown memory.

The church is the glory of Ashbourne, and we will, if it please you, pass in at the gates and down the gravelled walk, where the trained lime trees rise on either side, a wall of delicate green. A summer's day might be spent meditating among the green grasses and graves of this 'God's acre,' under the shadow of the crumbling walls and the gloom of the venerable yews. There is character to be studied, and histories to be traced in grave-mounds. There are tongues in tombs, and sermons in stones. Here, with a fresh offering of wild flowers, heavy with dew, is the grave of a little Nell; there, black with

ASHBOURNE

DIRECTORS INSPECT THE NEW LINE, DORE AND CHINLEY RAILWAY

THE GREEN MAN, ASHBOURNE

neglect, and dark with nettles, is the vault of a Scrooge. But we find but few neglected graves. The resting-places are bright with flowers. There a child's little grave is made radiant with roses, emblems of undying love; while a cluster of sweet-eyed Forget-me-Nots has been reverently laid on the next green mound.

The shadow of centuries falls upon us in the cool aisles of the church. The sacrilegious hand of the ecclesiastical 'restorer' has touched the fine old fabric of the church, but it has spared much that is ancient and interesting to antiquarians. If the dead who are buried here under the weight of marble monuments could be summoned, the town would be filled with a noble ancestry, with brave squires and stately dames, county kaisers and queens of hunt balls.

From the 'dim religious light' into the glad, green world again, with the sun shining hot and bright on the daisied grass, touching gently the white tombs, silvering the ripple of the cool brook, searching out the greys and greens and russets on roof and gable, and tinting the trees that bring the repose of woods into the very heart of the little town. The Senior (Wr)angler equipped with rod and landing net, creel, and live-bait can, and with his flies wound round his hat, is waiting for us impatiently at the Green Man, and wants to know what we have been mooning at, although before now he, too, has wandered within the shadowy precincts of that sacred church, and

WINSTER

come back better for his sweet, sad session of thought. Dove Dale is our destination now, and the talk is of trout, and in particular of a twenty-brace basket being taken in two hours yesterday with the floating Mayfly by a London barrister.

Edward Bradbury

READY FOR CHRISTMAS

The old brew-house was full of logs of wood, piled high against the walls, cut from trees which the wind had blown down. The coal-house with its strong ivied walls, part of the old fortress, had been stored with coal brought many a mile in the blaze of summer; twenty tons lay under the snow.

On the kitchen walls hung the sides of bacon and from hooks in the ceiling dangled great hams and shoulders. Bunches of onions were twisted in the pantry and barn, and an empty cow-house was stored with potatoes for immediate use. The floor of the apple chamber was covered with apples, rosy apples, little yellow ones, like cowslips balls, wizendy apples with withered, wrinkled cheeks, fat, well-fed, smooth-faced apples, and immense green cookers, pointed like a house, which would burst in the oven and pour out a thick cream of the very essence of apples.

Even the cheese chamber had its cheeses this year, for there had been too much milk for the milkman, and the cheese presses had been put into use again. Some of them were Christmas cheese, with layers of sage running through the middles like green ribbons.

Stone jars like those in which the forty thieves hid stood on the pantry floor, filled with white lard, and balls of fat tied up in bladders hung from the hooks. Along the broad shelves round the walls were pots of jam, blackberry and apple, from the woods and orchard. Victoria plum from the trees on house and barn, black currant from the garden, and red currant jelly, damson cheese from the half-wild ancient trees which grew everywhere, leaning over walls, dropping their blue fruit on paths and walls, in pigsty and orchard, in field and water trough, so that Susan thought they were wild as hips and haws.

Pickles and spices filled old brown pots decorated with crosses and flowers, like the pitchers and crocks of Will Shakespeare's time.

In the little dark wine chamber under the stairs were bottles of elderberry wine, purple, thick, and sweet, and golden cowslip wine, and hot ginger, some of them many years old, waiting for the winter festivities.

There were dishes piled with mince pies on the shelves of the larder, and a row of plum puddings with their white calico caps, and strings of sausages, and round pats of butter, with swans and cows and wheat-ears printed upon them.

111

BAKEWELL

Everyone who called at the farm had to eat and drink at Christmastide.

A few days before Christmas Tom Garland and Dan took a bill-hook and knife and went into the woods to cut branches of scarlet-berried holly. They tied them together with ropes and dragged them down over the fields, to the barn. Tom cut a bough of mistletoe from the ancient hollow hawthorn which leaned over the wall by the orchard, and thick clumps of dark-berried ivy from the walls.

Indoors Mrs Garland and Susan and Becky polished and rubbed and cleaned the furniture and brasses, so that everything glowed and glittered. They decorated every room, from the kitchen where every lustre jug had its sprig in its mouth, every brass candlestick had its chaplet, every copper saucepan and preserving-pan had its wreath of shining berries and leaves, through the hall, which was a bower of green, to the two parlours which were festooned and hung with holly and boughs of fir, and ivy berries dipped in red raddle, left over from sheep marking.

Holly decked every picture and ornament. Sprays hung over the bacon and twisted round the hams and herb bunches. The clock carried a crown on his head, and every dish-cover had a little sprig. Susan kept an eye on the lonely forgotten humble things, the jelly moulds and colanders and nutmeg-graters, and made them happy with glossy leaves. Everything seemed to speak, to ask for its morsel of greenery, and she tried to leave out nothing.

On Christmas Eve fires blazed in the kitchen and parlour and even in the bedrooms. Becky ran from room to room with the red-hot salamander which she stuck between the bars to make a blaze, and Margaret took the copper warming-pan filled with glowing cinders from the kitchen fire and rubbed it between the sheets of all the beds. Susan had come down to her cosy tiny room with thick curtains at the window, and a fire in the big fireplace. Flames roared up the chimneys as Dan carried in the logs and Becky piled them on the blaze. The wind came back and tried to get in, howling at the key-holes, but all the shutters were cottered and the doors shut. The horses and mares stood in the stables, warm and happy, with nodding heads. The cows slept in the cow-houses, the sheep in the open sheds. Only Roger stood at the door of his kennel, staring up at the sky, howling to the dog in the moon, and then he, too, turned and lay down in his straw.

In the middle of the kitchen ceiling there hung the kissing-bunch, the best and brightest pieces of holly made in the shape of a large ball which dangled from the hook. Silver and gilt drops, crimson bells, blue glass trumpets, bright oranges and red polished apples, peeped and glittered through the glossy leaves. Little flags of all nations, but chiefly Turkish for some unknown reason, stuck out like quills on a hedgehog. The lamp hung near, and every little berry, every leaf, every pretty ball and apple had a tiny yellow flame reflected in its heart.

Twisted candles hung down, yellow, red, and blue, unlighted but gay, and on either side was a string of paper lanterns.

SCARTHIN, CROMFORD

Margaret climbed on a stool and nailed on the wall the Christmas texts, 'God bless our Home', 'God is Love', 'Peace be on this House', 'A Happy Christmas and a Bright New Year'.

Scarlet-breasted robins, holly, mistletoe and gay flowers decorated them, and the letters were red and blue on a black ground. Never had Susan seen such lovely pictures, she thought, as she strained up and counted the number of letters in each text to see which was the luckiest one.

Alison Uttley

VILLAGE SHOPS

At Christmas, Mr. Green's own upstair parlour, where he sat to view the market-place on Sundays, or the roundabouts at the Fair, was transformed into a toyshop, and my mother and I went up the wooden stair, I in a flutter of excitement, as I smelled the odours of cardboard and tin, my mother talking happily as she lifted her dress from the dark steep way. I saw dolls and horses, trains and clockwork toys, and although none of them was for me, for my present was always a book, yet I tasted the joys of others. Downstairs he had Christmas cards, spangles and balls for kissing bunches, and from these we made a selection.

On November 5th his stock was pink masks, and big noses, bundles of tiny red Chinese crackers, rockets and Catherine-wheels. We always carried away a supply of these for my father to let off on the lawn.

On St Valentine's Day we beheld a collection of beautiful lace-frilled valentines. The servant boys bought comic ones, with big heads and little bodies. I felt uncomfortable when I looked at them, and shut my eyes to keep the sight away. I gazed longingly at the silver hearts pierced with arrows and scented with violets, but there was some mystery about them, whispering and blushing and teasing which I couldn't understand. It was something essentially grown-up, like having babies and going to rent dinners.

At Eastertide Mr Green had religious cards, and there I felt at home. I always bought a twopenny picture of a silver cross with some lilies or similar device for my mother, with the words 'The Lord is Risen'. As for Easter eggs, I never saw one in any of the village shops.

Mr Green with his pageant of seasonable toys, was a symbol of Santa Claus to my mind. He knew beforehand, and decided what we were to have; he arranged with some hidden powers the skipping season, the marble season, St Valentine's Day and Easter. He was never caught napping by spring or winter, he was always prepared with the special delights.

COTTON STREET, BOLSOVER

I had no idea he bought them himself, I imagined that he was the origin of these bounties, that he was rich with all the possessions in his shop. His life was my ideal, except that I wanted the toyshop at the top of our hill, inside the barn, where I would play all day. I had no desire to live in the village with its odours of limestone, of dust and the blacksmith's forge. When we drove off home, my heart rose in thankfulness for the rapid motion, the cold sweet air which rushed in my face, and the sounds of birds and the ruffling leaves around me.

Near Mr Green's shop was the tinsmith's, where stout Miss Kidd came to the tinkle of a little bell, and sold us lanterns and skewers, besoms, and baking-tins. If my mother were with us there was always a talk about Miss Kidd's health. She walked so slowly across the shop I felt she would never arrive, and I had all a child's impatience as I waited.

Then came Miss Budd the milliner. Only my mother and I entered that little shop, for my father flatly refused to meddle with fal-lals. If we were long choosing the ribbon velvet, or the flower, he whistled and rattled with the butt-end of his whip, hurrying us out. My new silk gloves came from Miss Budd's shop, and all our trimmings and furbelows. Miss Budd came forward, sprightly as a wren, with bright brown eyes and quick talk. She brought out her trays of flowers, and rolls of ribbons, and my mother looked at them, touching them with gentle, lingering fingers, wishing to spend a long time over the delight of choice, yet alarmed for my father's restiveness. There were sprays of jet, nid-nodding like quaking-grass, and jet buckles and bead-trimmings. She made her hasty decision, looking longingly at something else, but leaving it, as she

HADFIELD

114

ALL SAINTS, DERBY

clutched her paper bag and scurried down the steps to my waiting father.

At the top of the hill, the last shop in the village, was the butcher's, and there my father discussed the pedigree of the animal before he bought the meat.

'This is a prime bullock from Varley Hall,' said the butcher, or ''Tis a lamb from Mr Nettlefold's prize flock.' We paid the highest price and got the best, for I heard these discussions over again as I sat at table. 'He's dearer than any butcher in the county,' said they, 'but he only sells prime beasts. He won't buy any animal that isn't first class.' I was miserable at this, for it told me that the food I was eating was an acquaintance of mine. Later a 'foreign' meat seller opened a shop, for frozen meat. We thought this was the downfall of farming.

The boot-shop was next to the druggist's and the two shops were kept by the most important people in the village. They were independent, they had made money by careful and good trading, and some day they would retire to villas in the neighbouring town.

Alison Uttley

DERBYSHIRE INFIRMARY CONDEMNED

Sir,

The members of the Infirmary Saturday Committee, with a number of representative working men from the various firms

in Derby, by preconcerted arrangement, made a tour of inspection of the Derbyshire Infirmary on Saturday afternoon, March 14th, Mr Taylor, House Surgeon, acting as cicerone, their object being to ascertain by actual experience and personal observation what are the sanitary and other defects of the noble institution which has been of such vast and incalculable benefit to the town and county. Their attention was especially directed to the Nightingale wing, of which they made a careful and minute inspection. Most of them little thought what a 'whited sepulchre' they were to explore – fair on the outside, but inside dirty, foul-smelling and ill-lighted wards and corridors, in some portions of which the blessed sunlight was never seen; nurses' quarters warranted to slowly poison their unfortunate inmates; ventilation – surely a parody on the word, for of all the ingenious and intricate schemes to afford fresh air to the patients and staff the system that has been in vogue is about the worst that could be devised – as one of our number facetiously put it, 'the air only wanted directing where to go;' rotten deal floors that creaked at the tread, with ominous cracks and interstices, and that had absorbed the accumulated matters of past years; underneath the floors layers of dust containing Heaven knows what awful possibilities in the shape of microbes and germs, and a very paradise for rats; corridors that in the aggregate would extend to three-quarters of a mile in length, a great deal of which were perfectly useless, except to find work for charwomen.

The evils of the present structure were so patent to us that it was the subject of universal comment amongst us why the Infirmary had not been condemned years ago on account of its

CHESTERFIELD

innumerable structural and sanitary defects. As one somewhat irreverently said, 'It has been fearfully and wonderfully made.' Derbyites little know what an extraordinary place their local hospital is internally. A word or two in regard to the Nightingale block. We are fully convinced that any unbiassed and unprejudiced person, after examining it as carefully as we did, would endorse the opinion expressed by the whole of our number that – looking at it from any standpoint, structurally, architecturally, or financially – it would be supreme folly to retain it in the new contemplated institution.

Some of us had been somewhat sceptical in regard to the utility or otherwise of destroying the Nightingale wing, and we came away thoroughly converted to the opinion of the Building Committee – that it would be eminently unwise and impolitic to retain any portion of the present structure, and that the whole pile of buildings must be demolished, so that a new institution can be erected, one up to the present day requirements and workings of the town and county at large. We have not the slightest hesitation in saying that when the working classes are appealed to in this matter of so much vital concern and momentous interest to them, they will generously respond to the invitation, and will show by their contributions that they are determined that their refuge in times of accident or disease shall be the best, 'humanly speaking,' that can be devised.

At the close of our extremely interesting and profitable visit, Mr Bonnington (Midland Railway Carriage Works) on our part cordially thanked Dr Taylor for his courtesy in acting as our

BARTON'S QUARRY, LITTLE EATON

BAKEWELL

guide, and for the valuable information he had afforded us. Mr Keasley (of George Fletcher & Co.) then proposed: 'That this meeting of the Infirmary Saturday Committee and the other working class representatives here assembled, tender their best thanks to the Building Committee for the very satisfactory course they have pursued in the matter of a new Infirmary, and will gladly co-operate with them in their laudable efforts to erect an Infirmary worthy of the town and county.' This was seconded and carried unanimously, and a wish expressed that a notice should be conveyed to the press.

Yours truly,

H. Keasley.

W. Bonnington.

Derby Express, 17 March 1891

[Queen Victoria laid the foundation stone for a new hospital on 11 May 1891 and allowed the new name, Derbyshire Royal Infirmary. The new building was opened by the Duke of Devonshire on 7 July 1894.]

FARMHOUSE BATH NIGHT

We had no bathroom, nor had anyone else whom I knew, but we had baths. We possessed a fine collection of these, ranging from large flat round baths, which took up most of the floor surface of the little bedrooms, to high-backed oval baths, standing on four legs. They were white inside and grained brown and yellow outside, and very beautiful I thought they were. In the hay-barn next door to the cow-house was a hundred-year-old bath, very high, and long and narrow, like a sarcophagus. It was filled with Indian corn for the fowls, and we leaned perilously over the side with a dipper to draw up the maize, which lay like golden water in the white enamelled interior.

The largest hip bath, with a high moulded back and a hooded spout for emptying the water, was kept in the parlour bedroom for the use of the quality who sometimes honoured us. In the little bedroom which had lately been the cheese chamber, a small bath was used, a square high tub with four legs. One sat down very carefully lest it should overbalance and the contents flood the carpet. It was the warmest bath, for its sides kept away all draughts.

117

GIRLS' FRIENDLY SOCIETY, LITTLE EATON

The smallest bath was one left to us by a canon. The delightful old church dignitary used to stay with us for several weeks each year to compose his sermons and write his books. He brought his painted bath, a little chair and diminutive table with him. We kept them ready for his visits. When, after many years, he died, they were part of his bequest to us, and the little bath went with me to London.

These painted, polished baths that inhabited our house were familiar as human beings, and I felt a strong affection for them. I knew their idiosyncrasies – which bath was chilly and safe, which was warm but unsteady. One of them needed a great deal of water, so it was unpopular, and another was difficult to empty without spilling.

There was a humbler bath which was kept in the back kitchen for the occasional use of farm workers. The servant man carried it to his loft and bathed in it. The servant girl had her bath before the kitchen fire on Saturday nights when everyone had gone to bed. It was my own bath when I was very young, and it was a washtub too. It was called 'The Tin Pancheon', a dignified name, for it was round and high and large. I fitted into it like a snail in a shell, hidden by its high walls. The wide house doors were open to the yards, and the wind came rushing through the house nearly sweeping the naked bather out of the water.

A bath night was additional work for the servant girl but everyone was used to carrying water. A milk-can was filled from the drinking-water trough among the ferns and borne icy-cold to the bedroom. Another milk-can holding several gallons was half-filled with hot water from the kitchen copper-

pan. A bath sheet of great size and thickness was spread over the carpet and there were warning cries, 'Keep away! Are you ready?' as the bath was filled.

The steam circled in ghostly eddies, and the candle paled in the haze. In winter there was always a good fire alight on the bedroom hearth, and the bath was placed near. There one sat in the greatest contentment, with the dancing flames in the chimney, with the candle sending grotesque enormous shadows on the closely drawn tapestry curtains, and the cake of Pears' soap mingling its own intimate smell with the strong aromatic odour of the hot rain-water. That water came from the enormous wooden vats under the roof edge, where generations of elm leaves had fallen and decayed. The smell was a rich one, compounded of ferns and moss and vegetation. The woodland birds which bathed in the pools deep among the trees must have had the same kind of leafy smell as they splashed. A bath without that autumnal smell was no bath. And the softness of the water! It was like silk as it poured from the sponge and splashed over the sides to the floor. So there one sat, dreaming by the fire, unconscious of time, staring at the gold caverns and castles in the flames, listening to the wind as it beat against the strong walls of the farmhouse, and the creaking of the shutters and the cries of the owls. There one sat, blissfully naked, burning at the front, freezing at the back, dripping the hot water over one's body. Nobody knocked at the bathroom door, for it was private property. Nobody wanted to come in. The water could remain there till morning, when the servant girl would come after milking with her cans and carry it away, groaning over the weight, remarking that it

CHATSWORTH DAIRYMAID

wasn't worth having a bath if you couldn't make the water dirtier than that!

The water would be carried downstairs, through the kitchen, and used to swill the stone paths. In summer it would go to the rose trees and soak the roots of the Glory roses, or the cabbage roses on the old building. It wouldn't be wasted. There was a continuity about life, which made me part of all things, of water and trees and rain, and the bath-water soaked back into the earth, its home.

On the slender mahogany towel-rail beside the fire, sheltering the bath from the door, hung a bath-towel, as big as a sheet. It was one of the ancient towels which had been in the oak chest on the landing for fifty years before I was born. There in the corner was the date to prove it. It had the smell of lavender, and tansy, and camomile, sweet and bitter herbs strewed there, and also the smell of Pears' which was stored in the chest. The scent of that chest was so strong that everything inside was permeated with it, and it saturated the bath-towels. I dried by the fire, and slipped over my head my warm calico nightgown adorned with feather-stitching on its turned-down collar. Then a dash to the door, and out to the dark landing to call and call, to ring a brass bell, and call again, every moment getting colder, for there were no dressing-gowns or luxuries.

Noises came from downstairs, deep voices talking, rumbling laughter, somebody singing, the grandfather clock striking and drowning all else, chairs grating on stone floors, and outside a cow mooing in the Irishman's Place. At last my voice was heard, and a beam of light appeared.

Upstairs came my mother bearing a bowl of steaming bread and milk with a sprinkle of brown sugar, and nutmeg and thick cream on the top. That was to keep me from catching cold after the exposure of my bath.

I scrambled into the wide bed with its three or four feather mattresses piled so high that I sank into them as if into a snow-drift.

Alison Uttley

TRIPPERS

Castleton should be given a wide berth on a Saturday or Sunday in the summer months. On those days it overflows with the tripper, for whom it lays itself out to provide, and its streets are apt to be uproarious until the last brakes have gone singing down the vale. Its main thoroughfares are commonplace, but the cottages on the higher level are picturesque and unspoilt. Castleton retains one interesting local custom, for May 29th, or Oakapple Day, is still honoured in a curious way. A great garland of wild flowers is made, shaped like a bell on a frame, and is carried round the town by a man on horseback, who wears it upon his head, covering his face. He plays Charles II; the part of the Queen who rides beside him is taken by a youth, dressed in a lady's riding habit and veil.

CASTLETON

Twenty girls dance the Morris dance before them as they ride through the town to the accompaniment of 'plenty of brass bands.' One can conceive the din! Then the garland is taken to the church and slung up by a pulley to a parapet of the tower, where it is left to wither. It is accounted a great honour to bear the garland, and the privilege has been exercised by the same man for the last twenty years.

J.B. Firth

A NIGHT IN HAYFIELD

While I was sitting in the little bar-parlour of the 'Royal' that night, thinking of the strange dark trenches on the moors, a cattle-dealer and his man arrived, and forthwith called for ale. The ale disappeared in a twinkling, and the cattle-dealer put his empty glass down with a huge sigh, saying, 'It's a dree walk ower t' top.' He was a ponderous, broad-faced, heavy-jawed man, and as he sat on the bench his Falstaffian stomach touched the table. When he laughed he shook all over like a big jelly. His drover, on the other hand, was a lean and wiry-looking old fellow, with a grizzled beard, shaggy eyebrows, and a keen, knowing, cruel face. His voice was so deep and hoarse

that it seemed to issue from a cavern in the earth rather than out of a human throat. He was rather deaf, and required to be well shouted at before he picked up the meaning of anything addressed to him. These two worthies were evidently old acquaintances, and it soon appeared that the drover had recently come out of jail, where he had been spending thirty days in solitude, though not in idleness. 'I'd ha' paid his fine and the costs − £6 10*s* − ' said the dealer to me, 'only they'd soon ha' had him in agin. You know they divide them fines among 'em.'

'What, magistrates and all?' said I.

'Of course − so Jo served his time. Why, if he'd paid t' money they'd allus a' been nabbin' him. That's how they live, loike. Ask him what they sent him for.' I did so, but did not succeed in making myself heard. Then the cattle-dealer put the question in tones which sounded like a distant clap of thunder. All the glasses on the table seemed to shake with the reverberation.

'Genelman wants to know what they put thee in for, Jo?'

'Ay,' growled the drover; 'because at back eend o' t' year I jest gien a coo a clip ow' t'nose. It bleeded a little, and they tuk me.'

'Where did they put 'ee, Jo?'

'In Strangeways jail. Ay, but it was a cawld spot. But mazin' fine place, loike − the gates were so big yow'd thowt you were gine into Chatsworth Park. And sich kase (keys)! I went in t'

120

MAGPIE LEAD MINE, SHELDON

kara-wan, and there was a little light oop above about as big as a penny. It were a fine kara-wan, with a policeman sittin' on t' step. It went asy, loike.'

By 'kara-wan' he meant the prison van, and evidently did not use the word by way of burlesque, but because it seemed stately and grand, like the vehicle in which he was conveyed to the 'cawld spot.'

'There were a cobbler wi' thee, wasna theer?' roared the cattle-dealer.

'Ay, there wor that. His hair hung down his back like a coo's tail. He wor a' coovered wi' hair, oop an' doon.'

'What did do to him, Jo?'

'My word, they fetched pair of scissors half-a-yard long and clipt un. Ay, but he made a naze (noise). Then they made un get into t' feesh pond and wished (washed) him. They scroobed him wi' a big broosh, and he did yowl. He thowt he was drowndit.' By fish pond Jo meant the prison bath.

'How didst find thy bed, loike?' asked the fat dealer, who clearly knew all the story, but never could have enough of it.

'T' bed was a' oop on end, and in t' night yow coomed down off un', cloos an' all. There was nowt but a wooden pillow, and t' yead slipped down. It was awful cawld, too – and nowt to eat but dree bread. Yow couldna sleep for t' cawld.'

'What did t' do to cobbler, Jo?' bellowed the dealer, for this was the part of the story he liked best, and when the drover slackened up a little, this question instantly set him off again. 'Did t' wish him, Jo?'

'Ay, they did that, I tell 'ee. He wor all black, but they scroobed him with a big broosh, till t' feesh pond was all black wi' 's dirt. He wor covered wi' long hair, but they clipt un.'

The company thought it was very hard on Jo that he should be sent to prison, but his face belied him if he did not well deserve it. Indeed, the salesman whispered to me that he was 'mighty quick with his ash-plant,' – a big stick with a crooked handle which he carried in his hand. I am inclined to think that the journey in the caravan will do him good. But it may not be well for him to be kept in 'free drinks' every night while he spins his yarn. The cattle-dealer stood ale as fast as he wanted it, and long after I was in bed I heard him bellowing, 'Jo, what did t' do to cobbler?' and the hoarse tones of the drover describing how they clipt un and wished un i' t' feesh pond. Such were the voices of the night at Hayfield. Small as the town is, it is not a very quiet place at night; few small towns are.

Louis J. Jennings

LITTLEOVER HOLLOW, DERBY

Sources and Photographic Details

TEXT

The page numbers given below relate to pages in this book and not the page numbers of the source books.

Sources of the texts are as follows: The Amateur Angler *Dove Dale Revisted* pp. 28, 95; William Armstrong and J.E. Harborn *Buxton Waters, Baths and Accessory Methods of Treatment* p. 55; Edward Bradbury *All About Derbyshire* pp. 42, 107; Edward Bradbury and Richard Keene *All About Derby* p. 91; James Croston *On Foot Through The Peak* pp. 9, 24, 60, 82; J.B. Firth *Highways and Byways in Derbyshire* pp. 62, 89, 119; Louis J. Jennings *Rambles Among The Hills* pp. 12, 21, 26, 31, 49, 53, 54, 59, 82, 100, 103, 120; F.J. Metcalfe *Colliers and I* pp. 23, 69, 73; 'An Old Blue' *The Tale of Evam* p. 86; Joseph Sharpe *Dark By Seven* (Edit. Nellie Connole) pp. 13, 37, 75; Alison Uttley *Ambush of Young Days* pp. 17, 36, 45, 47, 66, 113, *Recipes from an Old Farmhouse* pp. 50, 77, 98; *A Country Hoard* pp. 111, 117 (all extracts from Alison Uttley courtesy of Faber and Faber).

Newspapers include *Derby Express* p. 115; *Derby Mercury* pp. 39, 50, 51, 81, 90, 93, 96, 104; *Derby Times* p. 65; *High Peak News* pp. 13, 71.

Manuscript source: F.W. Brocklehurst's reminiscences of his early life in the village of Sheldon, Derbyshire, deposited at The Museum of English Rural Life, University of Reading.

ILLUSTRATIONS

The credits and notes on the illustrations used in the book are given in page ascending order. Where a source is referred to frequently, initials only are used and a key to these abbreviations is given at the end of the section. When dates are known, or can reasonably be deduced, these are given. If the photographer is known the name is added in brackets at the end of the entry.

Endpapers: front, Children's party in John Else's field, Matlock *c.* 1911; back, Lumsdale Quarry, Matlock; Mr and Mrs F. Winfield. Title page i, Little Eaton woods, *c.* 1890; DLS. ii, View of Hathersage from Burbage; DLS. Gamekeepes at Calke Abbey at the time of Sir Vauncey Harpur Crewe *c.* 1900; Leslie Cox. Page iii, Photographer Hans Hansen of Ashbourne, 1890s (Hansen); DLS. Pierrot concert in the band-stand on Lover's Walk, Matlock Bath, *c.* 1900; TH. Page 1, Inside Treak Cliff Cavern, Castleton, *c.* 1900; DLS. Page 2, The Long Bridge, Stanton-by-Bridge *c.* 1900 (Martin); Geoff Heath. Luke Garside, a famous Hayfield character, around the turn of the century; Willow Publishing. Page 3, Lovers' Walk, Matlock Bath, 1880; DLS. Page 4, Chesterfield's famous twisted spire seen from St Mary's Gate *c.* 1900; David Roberts. Page 5, Cardplayers at 58, St John's St, Ashbourne, *c.* 1900; DLS. Visitors on the terrace at Smedley's Hydro, Matlock *c.* 1900 (Seaman); Beryl Edmonds. Page 6, Photographer, A. Seaman at Smedley's Hydro, Matlock, *c.* 1900; Beryl Edmonds. Page 7, Mrs Hansen, wife of the photographer, and their daughter, Ashbourne *c.* 1900; DLS. Page 9, Speedwell Cavern, Winnats, Castleton, *c.* 1909; DLS. Page 10, Church St, Castleton, *c.* 1909; DLS. Page

11, Peacock Hotel, Baslow, *c.* 1914 (renamed Cavendish Hotel 1974); CST, Speedwell Cavern; GC. Page 12, Via Gellia, *c.* 1900; DLS. Page 13, Masson Mill, near Cromford, *c.* 1900; Tony Bowker. Page 14, Two Dales, *c.* 1900; GC. Page 15, Children of the village school, Sheldon *c.* 1900; MERL. Page 16, Market at the Morledge, Derby, early 1900s; DLS. Page 17, Ockbrook Lodge with John Waswick and family, Ockbrook *c.* 1887; J Le C. Smith. Page 18, Tea in a garden near Lathkill Dale, *c.* 1905; DLS. Page 19, Sunday School class at Birchwood Chapel, Riddings; DLS. Mr Bagshaw, Matlock, reputed to have weighted 24 stones *c.* 1900; Mr and Mrs F. Winfield. Page 20, Loscoe Grange; DLS. Page 21, J.B. White and Sons, Burlington St, Chesterfield, 1894; DLS. Page 22, Glossop Fire-Brigade, 1900; DLS. Page 23, The Derwent Hotel, Whatstandwell; TH. Page 24, The Parade, Matlock Bath, 1891; DLS. Matlock Bath; DLS. Page 25, The Rutland Cavern (Old Nestor Mine), Heights of Abraham, Matlock Bath, early 1900s; TH. The Petrifying Well, Matlock Bath; Les Taylor. Page 26, Chatsworth Park; CST. Page 28, The Chatsworth Hotel, Chatsworth Park, now the Estate Offices; DLS. Page 29, Monsal Dale, 1890s; DLS. Fishing in the river Dove *c.* 1900; DLS. Page 30, Lion Face Rock, Dove Dale; DLS. Page 31, Thorpe Cloud and Dove Dale, 1891; DLS. Page 32, Tissington village *c.* 1900; DLS. Page 33, Bonsall village; TH. A quiet lane near Ashbourne *c.* 1900; DLS. Page 34, Lathkill Dale; GC. Page 35, Atlow Mill near Matlock, 1890s; TH. The Barley Mow, Kirk Ireton; TH. Page 38, High St, Bolsover; GC. Young miners descending the Denby Mine; Cliff Williams. Page 39, Denby Colliery officials, *c.* 1900; Sheila Tomlins. Page 40, Wirksworth Station; TH. Loading coal trucks at Denby Colliery *c.* 1900; DRO. Page 41, Market Place, Belper; DLS. White Lion Hotel, King St, Belper; Belper Historical Society. Page 43, Bonsall Cross; TH. Page 44, The Slack children, Middleton by Wirksworth; TH. Page 45, Gamekeeper's Cottage, Tywford *c.* 1900; Leslie Cox. Page 46, The Sunbeam Choir, Wirksworth; TH. Page 47, The Greyhound Hotel, Cromford; DRO. Page 48, Tufa Cottage, Via Gellia, 1891; DLS. Page 49, Bakewell, 1891; DLS. Page 50, South Church St, Bakewell, 1914; DLS. Page 51, Cornmarket, Derby, 1896; DLS. Page 52, The Cat and Fiddle, Buxton; Les Taylor. Goyt Valley, 1896; DLS. Page 53, Walkers at Kinder Clough, 1890s; Pam Gee. Page 54, The Crescent, Buxton; DLS. Page 55, Glossop Lamplighters; DLS. Attendants at St Ann's Well, Buxton dispensing the mineral waters; Les Taylor. Page 56, Bath St, Ilkeston; A.P. Knighton. Page 57, Quarndon *c.* 1905; DLS. Page 58, Sheldon village, 1890s; MERL. Page 59, Stony Middleton; TH. Page 60, The 'Plague Cottages', Eyam, 1919; DLS. Page 61, Plague commemoration service in Cucklet Delph, Eyam, early 1900s; GC, Edensor, Chatsworth; DLS. The Great Conservatory built by Joseph Paxton at Chatsworth, *c.* 1872; DLS. Repair work being carried out on the Great Conservatory at Chatsworth; CST. Page 63, The Victoria Regia House at Chatsworth with the kitchen garden staff posing, characteristically for the period, holding tools of their trade. On the right of the picture can be seen Joseph Paxton's house, *c.* 1905; CST. Page 64, Ben Stone, game-keeper at Chatsworth, early 1900s; CST. Page 65, The Duke of Devonshire's Shooting party at Chatsworth. The eighth Duke is left of cen-tre wearing check, early 1900s; CST. Page 66, Fife and Drum band at Whitfield near Glossop; DLS. Page 67, Shipley school, Miss Beechcroft and her class, 1905; DLS. Page 68, The Derbyshire Entomological Society on an excursion. Second from right on front row is Alison Uttley's school mistress, mentioned in her biography, 1890s; Sheila Tomlins. Page 69, Little Eaton wharf and the Clock House, lived in by the colliery manager at Denby, *c.* 1899; Sheila Tomlins. Page 70, Little Eaton wharf, loading coal into canal barges. The coal was brought from nearby Denby Colliery in horse-drawn trucks on a private railway line. The trucks containing the coal were then lifted off the bogeys and transported without tipping, 1897; Sheila Tomlins. Bakewell Mill, 1890s; Old House Museum, Bakewell. Page 71, The water-wheel that powered Masson Mill, Richard Arkwright's pioneering mill at Cromford; Tony Bowker. Page 72, Matlock Bath from above the fish-pond, 1870; DLS. The ferry across the Derwent at Matlock Bath, *c.* 1900; GC. Page 73, Wirksworth, *c.* 1900; TH. Page 74, Miners walking back to the ascending shaft at the end of a shift at the Clay Cross mine; Cliff Williams. John Wagg's bicycle shop at the corner of Bennett St and Derby Road, Sandiacre, *c.* 1908; DLS. Page 75, Miners returning home by coal truck from Shipley Colliery, *c.* 1900; DLS. Page 76, Miners and their families picking coal from waste-tips during the lock-out of 1893; Cliff Williams. Page 77, The annual rent meeting of tenant farmers at the Royal Oak, Ockbrook, 1898; J. Le C. Smith. Alec Lamb, who sold newspapers and fire wood in Codnor, *c.* 1900; DLS. Page 78, The wedding of G.H.M. Slack and Florence Byard at Bullbridge, 1909; W.H. Emmas-Williams. Ockbrook Lodge Private Day School. The Misses Waswick and the children, *c.* 1890; J. Le C. Smith. Page 79, High Street, Kings Newton, *c.* 1900 (Martin); Melbourne Civic Society. Market Place, Ashbourne, *c.* 1900 (Hansen); DLS. Page 80, Blackwell Bridge, Melbourne, *c.* 1900 (Martin); Melbourne Civic Society. Church Walk, Mayfield Road by St Oswald's Church, *c.* 1900 (Hansen); DLS. Page 81, A Bank Holiday in Matlock Bath. Compare this picture with the similar view taken on a quieter day on page 72, 1890s; TH. Market Day in Ashbourne, *c.* 1900 (Hansen); DLS. Page 82, Well-dressings at Hard's Well, Tissington. The bearded man on the right of the well is William Wright, blacksmith, *c.* 1899; MERL. Page 83, Twyford Ferry across the Trent, *c.* 1900; Leslie Cox. Haymaking at Calke Abbey, National Trust (Calke Abbey). Page 84, Kinder Scout looking towards Hayfield, *c.* 1900; Pam Gee. Bread delivery van at Hayfield; Pam Gee. Page 85, William Clough, Hayfield, *c.* 1900; GC. Page 86, The Square, Eyam, *c.* 1919; DLS. Page 87, Swarkestone church, *c.* 1900; Geoff Heath. Page 88, The Winnats, Castledon, 1909. DLS, Cottage at Grindleford, *c.* 1900; DLS. Page 90, Irongate and All Saints church, Derby, 1896; DLS. Page 91, Midland Railway Station, Derby; National Railway Museum. Page 92, Locomotive Depot, Top Yard, Derby, *c.* 1900; National Railway Museum. Refreshment waggon, Derby Station, *c.* 1908; National Railway Museum. Page 93, Ilkeston Station, early 1900s; A.P. Knighton. Page 94, Duffield, *c.* 1900 (Bland); DLS. Page 95, Part of celebrations for Queen Victoria's Jubilee in 1887 at Bradbourne; DLS. Page 96, Smedley's Hydro, Matlock, early 1900s; TH. The Conservatory at Smedley's Hydro, *c.* 1900 (Seaman); DLS. Page 97, The Castle gateway at Mackworth, near Derby, the only surviving portion of this late fifteenth century castle, *c.* 1890 (Keene); DLS. Page 98, The railway station at Little Eaton with paper mill in the background, *c.* 1900; Sheila Tomlins. Page 99, The 'Bird-Cage' Summer house or arbour, built in about 1706 by Robert Bakewell of Derby, in the gardens of Melbourne Hall, photograph early 1900s; Lord and Lady Ralph Kerr. Page 100, Chesterfield ice-cream seller by the Bull's Head Inn, Holymoorside, *c.* 1900; David Roberts. Page 101, Schoolgirls and May Day celebrations at Bolsover Castle, *c.* 1900; DLS. Page 102, Sheep shearing at Booth Farm, Kinder near Hayfield, John Marriott (left), John Needham (centre) and Esther Needham (right), *c.* 1899; Pam Gee. Page 103, The sheep wash near kinder, on the edge of Kinder Scout and Luke Garside, *c.* 1900; Pam Gee. Rebekah Marriott of Hill House, Kinder near Hayfield; Pam Gee. Page 104, Melbourne Hall, *c.* 1900; Lord and Lady Ralph Kerr. Page 105, Village of Ilam at the foot of Thorpe Cloud and close to Dove Dale, *c.* 1905; DLS. Page 106, The Devonshire Arms at Baslow, *c.* 1900; DLS. Page 107, The Avenue, Youlgrave, early 1900s; GC. Flood at Ashbourne, *c.* 1900 (Hansen); DLS. Page 108, Post Office at Bradbourne, *c.* 1900; TH. Shrove Tide Football game at Ashbourne, *c.* 1900 (Hansen) DLS. Page 109, Two Dales, near Matlock, *c.* 1900; GC. Gardener at Ashbourne, *c.* 1900 (Hansen) DLS. Page 110, The board of directors of the Dore and Chinley Railway inspect a new length of line, *c.* 1900; National Railway Museum. The Green Man and Black's Head Hotel, St Johns St, Ashbourne, *c.* 1900 (Hansen); DLS. Page 111, Winster, near Matlock, early 1900s; GC. Page 112, Bakewell viewed from the bridge, early 1900s; TH. Page 113, Scarthin, Cromford, part of the industrial hamlet and mill pond created by Richard Arkwright to supply people and power for his textile mills, photo-

graph early 1900s; TH. Page 114, Cotton St, Bolsover, *c.* 1900; DLS. Page 115, All Saints Church, Derby, 1896; DLS. Page 116, High St, Chesterfield, early 1900s; GC. Barton's Quarry, Little Eaton, early 1900s; Sheila Tomlins. Page 117, Children's Tea party in a garden in Bakewell, *c.* 1905; DLS. Page 118, The Girls' Friendly Society haymaking, Little Eaton, *c.* 1900; Sheila Tomlins. Page 119, Dairymaid weighing butter portions, Chatsworth House, *c.* 1900; CST. Page 120, Castleton, 1909; DLS. Page 121, Lead miners at the pit-head of Magpie Mine, Sheldon, *c.* 1900; MERL. Page 122, Littleover Hollow near Derby, 1890s; DLS.

KEY: CST, Chatsworth Settlement Trustees. DLS, Derbyshire Library Services. DM, Derby Museum. DRO, Derbyshire Record Office. GC, Gordon Coupe. MERL, Museum of English Rural Life, University of Reading. TH, Tony Holmes.